History Makers

A QUESTIONING APPROACH
TO READING AND WRITING BIOGRAPHIES

Myra Zarnowski

HEINEMANN
Portsmouth, NH

Heinemann
A division of Reed Elsevier Inc.
361 Hanover Street
Portsmouth, NH 03801–3912
www.heinemann.com

Offices and agents throughout the world

Library of Congress Cataloging-in-Publication Data
Zarnowski, Myra, 1945–
History makers : a questioning approach to reading and writing biographies / Myra Zarnowski.
p. cm.
Includes bibliographical references.
ISBN 0-325-00434-X
1. History—Study and teaching (Elementary)—United States. 2. Language arts (Elementary)—United States. 3. Biography as a literary form—Study and teaching (Elementary)—United States. I. Title.
LB1582.U5 Z37 2003
372.89—dc21
2002151527

Editor: Danny Miller
Production service: Denise Botelho
Production coordinator: Elizabeth Valway
Cover design: Lisa Fowler
Composition: Tom Allen, Pear Graphic Design
Manufacturing: Steve Bernier

Printed in the United States of America on acid-free paper
07 06 05 04 03 RRD 1 2 3 4 5

Contents

Acknowledgments

A big thank you goes to my dear friend Debbi Aizenstain who invited me into her classroom and allowed me to work with her students over the course of several years, winter school and summer school. This year Debbi worked with her students to complete their biographies—literally up until the very end—finishing the last books at 11:15 A.M. when school ended at 11:45.

Another thank you goes to Bill Varner who first suggested that I write this book. What I didn't know when I agreed was that this book wouldn't be a revision of my previous book, *Learning About Biographies*. It would be entirely different.

A large thank you goes to my editor, Danny Miller, who good naturedly read each chapter as it was written, made thoughtful comments, and gently urged me to finish.

Finally, a thank you to my husband Eddie for support and good humor. There's never too much of that.

1
A Questioning Approach to Biography
Putting Interpretation in the Forefront

W*hat* makes teaching history so hard, and what can we do about it? Why are adults willing to spend years researching the past with enormous enthusiasm, while children find even small doses of history (to use their favorite term) "boring"? These were the questions I confronted more than fifteen years ago when I first began working with children in New York City public schools to try to turn this situation around. As a result of my experiences, I wrote a book called *Learning About Biographies: A Reading-and-Writing Approach for Children* (1990) in which I shared my work with elementary and middle school students who assumed the role of biographer. As biographers, they read, discussed, researched, and wrote books about their subjects, putting their original interpretations on the facts. It was a successful and rewarding endeavor. It proved to me that when given time to dig into the past and to reflect on their learning, children could accomplish a great deal. More importantly, they enjoyed the process, and many were eager to do it again.

More than ten years later, I decided to revisit this work for several reasons. In the span of ten years following the book's publication, a number of teachers had tried out the strategies I recommended and made interesting and useful adjustments to the procedures. Chief among them were Tarry Lindquist and Walter Parker. In Tarry's book *Ways That Work: Putting Social Studies Standards into Practice* (1997), she adapted my approach to writing biographies and created what she called *cooperative biographies*. She had groups of children working together to complete the various chapters in an original biography. Walter Parker, too, in his textbook *Social Studies in Elementary Education* (2001) took up the idea of cooperative biographies and, once again, offered some new ideas. I have learned from their work. After more than ten years, I think the time is right to revisit the ideas I once found so promising. It is an opportunity to add to that work some additional strategies based on current scholarship and my own teaching experiences. *A Questioning Approach to Biography* incorporates some of the earlier work, but also adds to it. Once again, I am eager to revisit the process of using biography with children.

An Intriguing Balance: Finding Out the Facts and Interpreting What They Mean

As I have found in the past and continue to find now, teaching history in the elementary and middle schools presents us with a unique challenge. On the one hand, our students have huge gaps in their background knowledge and conceptual understanding of the past. Here is an example of what I mean. Recently, I worked with sixth graders reading *Through My Eyes* (1999) by Ruby Bridges, a book in which the author tells us how as a six-year-old child she integrated an all-white elementary school in New Orleans. To successfully read this book, it was necessary for my students to understand what is meant by *segregation, integration, "separate but equal," Brown v. Board of Education, NAACP, federal marshals, Ku Klux Klan* and more. They needed to know about the political and social conditions in the 1960s because this was the context of Ruby's world. Building this background of concepts and context required effort—theirs and mine.

On the other hand, despite the gaps in their understanding, these children were capable of original thinking about the past—thinking we might call creative, constructive, and thoughtful. When thinking about what happened to Ruby Bridges, my students questioned many aspects of the events surrounding school integration. Why did Ruby's father, known as a reliable worker, lose his job? What prompted a few white parents to send their children to school, and why didn't the stories of these children—who also faced threats and angry crowds—receive the same attention as Ruby's? What happened to cause an abrupt change between Ruby's first year at the William Frantz School when she faced jeering crowds every day and her second year when the school was integrated without protest? These intriguing questions prompted discussion and writing that in no way resembled a simple retelling of remembered facts. Instead, responses were passionate, engaged, and original.

As a result of this experience and others like it, the question remains: How can we support this type of original thinking and at the same time fill in the huge gaps in our students' fund of information? The answer I suggest in this book is to use a *questioning approach*. This approach draws children closer to the discipline of history because it taps the kinds of questions historians ask and requires the kind of sense making that historians practice. It also provides time for filling in informational gaps. This delicate balancing act has been described as "absorbing and doing" (Parker, 2001) because students do two fundamental and complementary activities: they learn information by reading a mix of primary and secondary sources, and they engage in historical sense-making by exploring original interpretations of the facts.

Historians practice a specialized form of sense-making that starts with asking questions about available information: What don't I understand? What is confusing? What do I need to know more about? How did this happen? Why did this happen? This question-asking behavior, called "cultivating puzzlement" (Wineburg, 1999, p. 497), is what starts historians thinking about possible explanations and interpretations. It opens up new paths to explore, new ways of seeing. It is not only productive, it is "an act that engages the heart" (Wineburg, 1999, p. 497) because it can involve emotions such as shock and surprise, or amazement and awe as students respond to the facts. Cultivating puzzlement means that historians don't think of history as a timeline of what happened—a "one-way street" (Shemilt, 2000, p. 87) that leads from the past to the present with only one possible route. They think of history as open to a range of interpretations, some of which are more defensible than others.

Of course children cannot think with the depth of adult historians, but they can move toward a more mature understanding of the past. By giving them the tools of the historian, we can counter their tendency to engage in what has been called "fanciful elaboration" (VanSledright & Brophy, 1992), or just plain making up the details of history. However, fanciful elaboration is not just something children do. It is very much alive in the work of adult writers who believe that "rounding the corners to make a better narrative" is acceptable in nonfiction (Carvajal, 1998; Zarnowski, 2001). To counter this very human tendency to fill in the blanks of history, we can provide students with a clearer picture of evidence-based history and the role of historians in assembling it.

The questioning approach to biography explained in this book is one way to begin. Since this approach takes time and effort—more time and effort than required in reading a textbook and answering the questions in the back—the payoff for students and teachers must also be greater. Here are the reasons that I think it is:

- It's interesting. It's much more interesting to ask questions and put forth new ideas than it is to mimic and memorize someone else's. In addition, the process of asking and answering questions about biography gives students voice, enabling them to speak for themselves. They tell us what they think and why. This is something middle school students like to do.

- It provides a truer picture of historical knowledge. Knowledge about the past—whether it is a single person's history or the history of a particular time and place—isn't static. It can change over time as historians sift, shape, see, and re-see their material. When a single interpretation is considered as "our heritage," or as "the best story about the past" (Seixas, 2000, p. 21)—even when this story is a gripping narrative—students miss the opportunity to engage in historical thinking because someone else has already done the thinking for them. Students who write their own interpretations about the past understand that the past is still open to dialogue and debate and that they can contribute to the discussion.

- It meets the NCSS Standards. In *Children and Their World* (2002), David A. Welton's new social studies text for teachers, he notes that writing original biographies meets the standards of the National Council for the Social Studies, both in terms of the skills that students should acquire and the "powerful" social studies activities they should take part in. Among these skills are learning and manipulating information, constructing knowledge, and working with others; among the "powerful" social studies activities are those that are meaningful, integrative, challenging, and active. Although Welton was specifically commenting on writing cooperative biographies—original biographies written by small groups of children—his comments are also true for the other biography-related activities described in this book. Reading and writing biography (or writing critically about biography) will help students meet NCSS standards.

- It introduces children to quality nonfiction literature. We are fortunate, indeed, to have well-written biographies that can introduce children to some of the world's most interesting people. Recent subjects of children's biography include Sir Ernest Shackleton, Eleanor Roosevelt, FDR, Martha Graham, Sigmund Freud, Joan of Arc, William Shakespeare, Galileo, Michelangelo, Mahatma Gandhi, Malcolm X, Elizabeth I, Samuel Adams, Sojourner Truth, and more. We have biographies of the less famous too—Mary Anning (fossil hunter), "Snowflake" Bentley (developer of a technique for photographing snowflakes), Mary Kingsley (traveler in unexplored parts of Africa) and Jean-François Champollion (decipherer of Egyptian hieroglyphs), Gertrude Ederle (first woman to swim the English Channel), and John Stetson (creator of the Stetson hat). These books give young readers a chance to see how people dealt with the issues of their times.

The Appeal of Biography

As a life story, a biography tells readers how a person navigates the extremes of success or failure, riches or poverty, happiness or sadness, innovative change or stagnant sameness, determination or aimlessness. But biographies do more than deal with specific, personal stories. They also provide readers with an entryway to the larger issues of history. Anyone who reads a biography learns about the time and place in which the subject lived—the larger social, political, and economic factors of the time. Biographies raise questions that affect the larger society—issues of war and peace, change, citizenship, human rights, use of resources and technology, and more.

High quality biographies also provide models for student writing. More and more frequently, biographers are telling young readers the sources of their information, the steps they have taken to insure the accuracy of their material, their thoughts about the people they are writing about, and additional thoughts about the illustrations they include. As students read well-written biography, they have the opportunity learn about the craft of writing it—how a writer introduces a "big idea" or generalization, provides background information, integrates pictures and other visual information, allows for other interpretations and points of view, includes primary source material, acknowledges gaps in existing information, and credits sources of information. Well-written biographies are storehouses of examples of excellent nonfiction writing. Nothing helps a nonfiction writer more than reading quality nonfiction literature.

Looking Ahead

The next several chapters deal with ways of questioning and dialoguing with biographies. These include strategies such as *what if?*, a means of exploring how it might have been . . . but wasn't; *powerful pairs, triplets, and quads*, a careful examination of competing or complementary biographies about the same person; *visible authors*, a look at how authors put themselves into their biographies by telling us their "take" on the facts; and *sidebars, captions, timelines, and authors' notes*, ways of providing information to enhance the main text. In each case, examples from children's literature and questions related to the discipline of history are the ingredients of effective teaching strategies.

This book also makes use of some seemingly simple questions that form the basis for critically examining biography. They are: *What if? What's the difference? What do I think?* and *What else?* As you will see, applying these questions to the study of specific biographies leads to some complex and intriguing answers.

2
"What If?" History

A*sking* "What if?" offers us the intriguing possibility of considering how history might have been. How would things have turned out if one decision had been made instead of another? What if Ben Franklin's father allowed him to go to sea instead of apprenticing him to his brother who was a printer? What if Michelangelo listened to his father and rejected art as an occupation unfit for the son of a gentleman? The results would send successive events off in another direction. History would be quite different. Asking "What if?"—also referred to as "alternative history," "after-dinner history," "speculative history," "counterfactual history," "hypothetical history," and just plain "historical supposes"—is entertaining and engaging. Called "the historian's favorite secret question" (Cowley, 1999, p. xi), it has been recently rediscovered and popularized through a number of books, journal articles, and websites.

How come this intriguing pastime has not been shared more often with children? Steve Tally, author of *Almost America* (2000), a book devoted to speculative scenarios in American history, suggests why. Historians, according to Tally, fear that we—children and adults—don't know enough "real history" in the first place to start mixing it up with "might-have-beens." If we don't know the basics of history, they argue, how can we speculate about it? Why further blur the already blurry line between fact and fiction?

What is to be gained? Besides being amusing and entertaining—something in short supply in much history teaching and learning—"what if" history shows us that history is not predetermined. It didn't have to happen the way it did. Choices were made. Asking "what if?" gives us a sense of the chaos of the actual lived-through experiences (Ferguson, 1999). This sense of chaos is something we lose sight of when we see history as a linear, tightly packaged, one-way narrative. Believing that one event simply led to another is a flawed way of understanding the complexity of historical cause and effect. Because of our knowledge of how things did turn out, we lose sight of the fact that they didn't have to turn out as they did. Historians refer to this as *hindsight bias.* It's quite easy to think of history as a locked-in, unbreakable chain of events that consists of "this happened . . . and then this happened . . . and then this happened," and so on. Life, however, isn't that simple.

Another reason we don't introduce questions like "what if" is that we have heard myths about children's "readiness" for certain activities: Wait until children are ready to write (presumably after they can read and know the letters of the alphabet); wait until children are ready to read for information (presumably after they have learned to fluently read the words). These are worse than misguided ideas. They shortchange children intellectually. Children who do not experience thought-provoking reasons for reading and writing from the start are robbed of the opportunity of developing real life interests in literacy in general and history in particular. From my experiences with intermediate grade children, I know that they are ready and eager for challenges like asking "what if?" They can learn the necessary background history *and* question it too.

Doing "What If?" History in the Classroom

Focusing on Biography

Biography is a particularly useful type of literature for dealing with the question "what if?" Using biography, it's easy to determine the turning points in a life story—the times when a person made a decision that affected the rest of his or her life. Once we identify these decisions, we can ask, "what if?" What if a different decision had been made? Biographies put the individual person in the forefront of the narrative and the larger historical context in the background, so it easy to follow the course of events in a person's life and spot the decisions.

Picture book biographies offer many examples of decision making. *Only Passing Through: The Story of Sojourner Truth* (Rockwell, 2000) highlights the "transformation" of a slave girl named Isabella, who through a combination of will, determination, and conviction decided to change herself into a powerful spokesperson against the evils of slavery. *Passage to Freedom: The Sugihara Story* (Mochizuki, 1997) deals with the decision of Chiune Sugihara, the Japanese consul in Lithuania, to issue visas to

Jewish refugees escaping from the Nazis and certain death. He did this against the orders of his government and placed himself and his family in danger. Full-length biographies, too, are full of decision making. *Ida B. Wells: Mother of the Civil Rights Movement* (Fradin & Fradin, 2000) documents Wells' decisions to fight for civil rights and to wage a fierce campaign against lynching. *Pick & Shovel Poet: The Journeys of Pascal D'Angelo* (Murphy, 2000) documents the stubborn determination of an Italian immigrant to become a poet.

As we read biographies with students, we can work with them to identify these important decisions. We can ask, "What was decided? Why is this decision a turning point? How did it affect the course of this person's life? What if a different decision had been made?"

Biography, in addition, teaches us about historical context. It shows us that the world in which the person made decisions was different from our own. As many historians are quick to point out, people from the past are *not us* talking, dressing, eating, and behaving in funny ways. Instead, people are influenced by their times. We cannot directly put ourselves into the shoes of Sojourner Truth, Chiune Sugihara, Ida B. Wells, Pascal D'Angelo, or anyone else without understanding the times in which they lived. Because the events we are examining when we read a biography occurred in a setting different from our own, it's important not to judge people from the past as if they lived in today's world. Instead, we need to ask, What were the social and political constraints at that time? What were the customs and beliefs?

If we judge people from the past by our own standards of conduct or morality, we are engaging in a practice known as *presentism*. This is a difficult pitfall to avoid. Recently I read in the newspaper about the charges against Yale University for naming buildings and otherwise honoring past benefactors who were slave owners (Wieneck, 2001). While one side of this argument claims that slavery can never be morally defensible and those involved in it should be condemned not honored, the other side claims that that's just the way it was back then—wealthy people either owned slaves or somehow were involved with and profited from slavery. No matter which side of the argument we think is correct, we can begin early on to alert children to the fact that although we might share common bonds with people from the past, we do not live in their world, and we do not always think the same way. Discussing biographies can help us highlight these differences between past and present.

Children are less likely to encounter this mismatch between past and present perspectives when reading historical fiction. There is evidence that authors "snip away the less attractive pieces of the past to make their narratives meet current social and political preferences" (MacLeod, 1988, p. 27). In *Sarah, Plain and Tall* (MacLachlan, 1985), an unmarried woman answers a newspaper advertisement for a wife placed by a midwestern farmer during the late 1800s. Not only does she travel alone from New England to meet him, she lives unchaperoned in his house, behavior that is "uncharacteristic of [the] time and place" (MacLeod, 1998, p. 28). Similarly, in *The True Confessions of Charlotte Doyle* (Avi, 1991) which takes place in 1831, Charlotte, the teenage heroine, travels alone on a ship from Europe to America, becoming—after many harrowing adventures—the captain of the ship. This is a story one critic labeled as "preposterous" (MacLeod, 1998, p. 29). As we share stories such as these with children, we need to critically examine the historical context, paying attention to customs and ideas of the times.

Raising Questions About Decision Making

To put "what if?" history into practice, I worked with sixth graders who had read the story of Ruby Bridges in *Through My Eyes* (Bridges, 1999). After some initial discussion focusing on the 1960s and the civil rights movement in general, we focused on Ruby's story—how she had taken a difficult test that qualified her to integrate an all-white school, how the state of Louisiana tried to prevent and then stall the integration of its schools, and how the NAACP had persuaded the Bridges family to involve Ruby in the integration process.

Students were deeply moved by the story of a small girl who faced hostile crowds daily. They were intrigued by the close relationship that developed between Ruby and her white teacher, Mrs. Henry, as the two spent each school day together. Their caring relationship was in stark contrast to the daily hostility they both faced.

Two questions guided me as I pursued "what if?" history in the classroom:

- What are the **turning points** in the biography? These are the times when important decisions were made.
- **What if** a different decision had been made?

The first question focuses attention on identifying decisions that had an impact on historical outcomes. Focusing on these decisions highlights the importance of people as decision-makers. Sometimes the decision maker is the subject of the biography (in our case, Ruby Bridges) and sometimes it is other people (in our case, Ruby's parents, her teacher, the judge who ordered the Louisiana schools to integrate, and others). The second question invites consideration of the options—"the roads not taken." Here is an opportunity to show that history is not a predetermined, inevitable story.

In order to make the search for "what if?"s as clear as possible, I gave the students a chart like the one in Figure 2–1 so that they could collect their ideas about both of these questions while reading. Using this chart, as a class we then made a joint list of all the turning points we found in Ruby Bridges' life. This list, reproduced in Figure 2-2, shows that the students could, indeed, identify many of the decisions that impacted Ruby's life. We also shared some of their initial ideas about possible *what if* scenarios, one of which they would develop in greater depth.

Exploring History by Writing About "What If?"s

The students then used the list of turning points as the basis of more in-depth writing. They each selected one turning point and explored this decision and the "what if?" possibilities that surrounded it. First, students wrote about the decision—the *who? what? where? when?* and *why?* of it. They made an effort to fill in as much background as possible for their readers—in this case, other sixth graders—who didn't know Ruby's story. Having a specific audience in mind was clearly helpful. Second, after describing the decision, students then explored its "what if?" possibilities.

It is important to stress the idea of plausible or believable alternatives as opposed to way-out ideas such as intervention by creatures from space, superheroes or technology that wasn't available at the time. If students do suggest implausible alternatives—ideas that are *not* accurate for the time—direct them to photographs and written material that explain the historical context. Ask them to examine this material closely in order to reevaluate what they have written. Working with a partner, students can read each other's work, to see if their "what if?"s are plausible.

Like professional writers who explore "what if?", our goal is always to suggest alternatives that would have been "seen at the time as realistic" (Ferguson, 1999, p. 88), are "based on the decisions of human beings, not acts of God" (Tally, 2000, xii), and are "surprising, entertaining, and occasionally frightening—but at all times plausible" (Cowley, 1999, xiii). In terms of the story of Ruby Bridges, this meant considering decisions that realistically could have been made by Ruby, her parents, her teacher, the parents of students who normally attended the William Frantz School,

FIGURE 2–1 What If? Data Chart

Ruby Bridges/Through My Eyes

People often make decisions that change the rest of their lives. In biography, these decisions are called *turning points* because they influence how a person's life turns out.

In Ruby Bridges' life, there were a number of turning points. Select a few turning points and for each one ask yourself, What if a different decision had been made? What are some possible—not "way-out"—results of that decision?

Turning Points (What important decisions changed Ruby's life?)	**What if?** (What if a different decision had been made? For each turning point, list another possible decision and then describe the effects of this decision.)
1.	1.
2.	2.
3.	3.

FIGURE 2–2 List of Turning Points

Turning Points: What important decisions were made that influenced the life of Ruby Bridges *and* changed the course of history?

- Ruby's parents moved to New Orleans.
- Ruby took a test in kindergarten.
- The NAACP convinced Ruby's parents to send her to an all-white school.
- Judge J. Skelly Wright forced two white public schools to integrate.
- Some white parents did not send their children to school.
- Dr. Coles became a part of Ruby's life.
- Mrs. Henry agreed to teach in an integrated school.
- The owner of the service station where Ruby's father worked fired him after customers complained that his daughter went to a white school.
- Protesters tried to stop integration.
- In spite of the protesters, four white children decided to attend the Frantz school.
- Norman Rockwell decided to paint a picture of Ruby going to school.
- John Steinbeck wrote about Ruby in *Travels with Charley*.
- People from around the world supported Ruby's family by sending letters, toys, clothes, and money.
- Mrs. Henry threatened the principal that she would call the superintendent if she didn't allow Ruby to play with the few white children at school.
- Mrs. Henry moved back to Boston. Protesters stopped after the end of Ruby's first-grade year.

federal judges and marshals, other citizens of New Orleans, and people throughout the world who learned about what was happening.

Some samples of the children's writing show that "what if?" was truly a productive question. Mario's discussion of Ruby's mother's decision to have her take the test is part of a complex situation involving the state's resistance to integration (see Figures 2–3 and 2–4). His probing of "what if?" possibilities begins by undoing the series of events that followed Ruby's passing the test that would determine her role in history. He suggests, instead, that she did not take the test at all. Then he "takes away" the

FIGURE 2–3 Mario's "What If?s"

FIGURE 2–4 Mario's "What If?s"

NAACP CONVINCES RUBY'S PARENTS TO SEND HER TO AN ALL WHITE SCHOOL.

That summer, Lucille Bridges and Abon Bridges were contacted by the NAACP (The National Association For The Advancement of Colored People). The NAACP is an old and well respected Civil Rights Organization. In the Spring of 1960, over one hundred black kindergarteners were given a special test by the school board. Several people from the NAACP came to Ruby's house that summer and told her parents that Ruby was one of just a few black children to pass the school board test. Ruby Bridges was chosen to go to an all white school; The William Frantz Elementary School.

Representatives from the NAACP told Ruby's mother and father it was a better school, and much closer to her home than the one she was going to. The NAACP said that Ruby has a right to go to a white school.They made a lot of promises such as giving her protection to and from school, if she needs it, giving her clothing to wear to school and telling her parents this school was much closer to her home. They pressured Ruby's mother and father by telling them it was her right to get a better education and she would lead the way for other black students.

FIGURE 2–5 Sammy's "What If?s"

FIGURE 2–6 Sammy's "What If?s"

subsequent events: there's no integration, no Mrs. Henry (Ruby's white teacher), no "equal" educational opportunity for blacks and whites. Finally, he suggests another fork in the road. Ruby's parents could have avoided this intensely painful situation altogether if the family had moved up North.

Sammy's "turning point" discussion begins with the efforts of the NAACP to convince Ruby's parents to send her to the William Frantz Public School (see Figures 2–5 and 2–6, pages 16 and 17). He talks about how representatives not only promised support but also made convincing arguments about why Ruby should go there. Like Mario, in his "what if?" Sammy suggests that Ruby might not have taken the test, but then he goes further. He suggests the possibility that representatives of the NAACP were not able to convince the family that Ruby should attend the William Frantz school. He understands the crucial role played by one little girl and her family.

Monique identifies Mrs. Henry's acceptance of a teaching job at the William Frantz Public School as an important "turning point" (see Figures 2–7 and 2–8). Acknowledging the immense impact this teacher made on Ruby, she lists many "what if?" possibilities that would have followed if Mrs. Henry had declined the job. While none of these possibilities is pursued, Monique is able to find many openings in the story where important decisions were made.

In the classroom, we compiled our collection of "what if?"s dealing with the story of Ruby Bridges into a book. This book, modeled on those written by historians—for example, *What If? The World's Foremost Military Historians Imagine What Might Have Been* (Cowley, 1999)—is an example of doing history in a way that historians do it. Just like well-known historians David McCullough, Stephen E. Ambrose, and James M. McPherson, my students and yours can learn more history by asking "the historian's favorite secret question" (Cowley, xi). We don't need to wait.

Examining "What If?"s in Children's Literature

While working on "what if?"s with students, it's helpful to share with them how published writers use this questioning strategy as well. Karen Cushman, author of many well respected works of historical fiction such as *Catherine, Called Birdy* and *The Midwife's Apprentice*, claims that "most of my stories start 'what if . . .' " (2001, p. 99). Referring to *Catherine, Called Birdy,* she recalls thinking, "What if there was this independent spirit who was at odds with her family and her society's desire to control her and use her for economic gain?" (p. 99). This is the intriguing and productive beginning of a work that won the Newbery Honor Award.

TURNING POINT

MONIQUE CURRIN

Mrs. Henry moves back to Boston

Mrs. Henry, a teacher, and her husband moved to New Orleans. The Henry's had moved because Mr. Henry's job transferred him to New Orleans from Boston.

One day, the Superintendent of Schools called Mrs.Henry to ask her if she would mind teaching an integrated class. Mrs. Henry replied, " Of course not". He gave her the assignment at The William Frantz Elementary School, where she would be teaching a little black six-year old girl name Ruby.

Many people protested against what Mrs. Henry was doing. All year the crowds protested every time Ruby and other white children entered The William Frantz School. As the year passed, the crowds stopped gathering around the school, and white mothers allowed their children to go back to school.

During the year, Mrs. Henry came to learn that there were other first graders in the school, but the principal had refused to let the other white first graders play with Ruby. Mrs. Henry thought this was not fair; they're all in the first grade.

Mrs. Henry demanded that the principal let them visit Ruby once or twice a day. The principal disagreed, but Mrs. Henry said she would call the Superintendent and address him about what she has been doing. Right away the principal agreed to let the white children play with Ruby because she knew what she was doing was against the law. Once or twice a day three white children would come to visit Ruby in her classroom and play.

Mrs.Henry had a big impact on her life. The more time Ruby spent with Mrs. Henry, the more she would act like her. Ruby was hoping Mrs. Henry would be her second grade teacher, but Mrs. Henry had moved back to Boston because the teachers did not like her and the principal did not want her to work at the school anymore. Ruby would never forget her teacher and Mrs. Henry would not forget about Ruby.

FIGURE 2–7 Monique's "What If?s"

WHAT IF....?

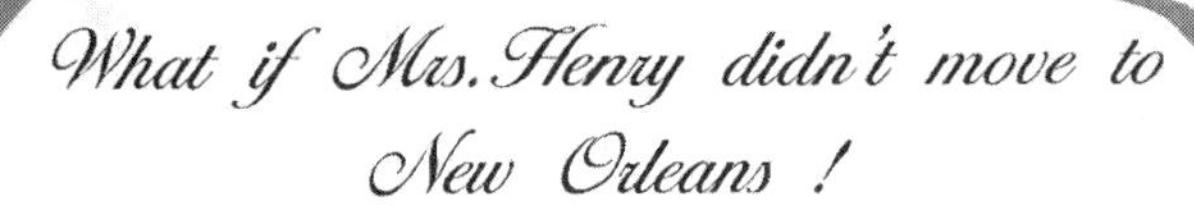

What if Mrs. Henry didn't move to New Orleans because her husband's job did not transfer him there?

What if the Superintendent couldn't get anyone to teach Ruby?

What if he offered one of the teachers triple the salary she was getting paid and she was just doing it for the money?

What if Ruby's teacher did not pay attention to her and made Ruby sit in the back of the classroom and told Ruby not to talk to her?

What if the teacher decided to fail Ruby at the end of the semester because Ruby didn't learn anything?

FIGURE 2–8 Monique's "What If?s"

"What if?" is used extensively in history and biography, too, as a productive strategy for questioning the past. Jerry Stanley's Orbis Pictus Award-winning book *Hurry Freedom* (2000) tells the story of Mifflin Gibbs, a black man who went to California during the gold rush of 1849, despite the fact that blacks weren't welcomed there. Stanley details the acts of hostility blacks faced as they moved to the West, and then raises specific questions about Gibbs' decision to go to California:

> An informed person, like Mifflin Gibbs, knew that the West was extremely hostile toward African Americans. They were barred from entering Indiana, Illinois, Kansas, and Oregon. To enter Ohio, Michigan, or Iowa, they had to post a bond of up to a thousand dollars. The western states and territories wanted an all-white population and granted few rights to African Americans. Even where there weren't laws against them, they wouldn't be welcome as competitors. To add to the uncertainty, California wasn't a state yet. *What if it became a slave state? What if it became a free state but barred African Americans from entering?* [emphasis added]. (p. 7)

These questions lead into the author's explanation of why Gibbs made this seemingly irrational decision. The "what if?"s help us understand the context of this situation so that we can appreciate Gibbs' decision, one that the author refers to as stemming from "hope born of desperation" (p. 7).

Diane Stanley and Peter Vennema's picture book biography *Cleopatra* (1994), an Orbis Pictus recommended title, presents a more favorable view of Cleopatra than many of us are used to reading. In fact, they tell us that one of the reasons she is seen so negatively is that the only surviving information we have about her was written by her enemies. After chronicling Cleopatra's amazing story, these authors suggest that it could have ended differently:

> She [Cleopatra] had ruled Egypt for twenty-one years and, having raised her country to new heights, had brought about its downfall. In a world where women had little power, she had fought to control the destiny of nations. *And if she had succeeded in her great venture, it would have been Cleopatra and her descendants who ruled the Western world, instead of the Emperors of Rome* [emphasis added]. (unpaged)

By ending the book this way, readers are encouraged to think about this situation and to speculate about how it might have turned out if Cleopatra had succeeded. Diane Stanley has ended several of her books by suggesting alternative endings and raising questions for readers. At the end of *Leonardo da Vinci* (Stanley, 1996), she makes this comment about his notebooks: "It is frustrating to imagine how the development of science and technology might have been advanced *if only* his work had been published" [emphasis added] (unpaged). Such endings are worth studying because they leave the reader speculating.

In *What's the Deal? Jefferson, Napoleon and the Louisiana Purchase* (1998), an Orbis Pictus recommended title, Rhoda Blumberg tells readers:

> The Louisiana Purchase was not inevitable.
>
> The history of North America would have been different had Napoleon decided to keep Louisiana.
>
> *There could have been other outcomes* [emphasis added] (p. 116).

Blumberg then provides five of these other possible outcomes, suggesting for example, that Napoleon might have decided to increase the French population of Louisiana so that it could wage war against its U.S. neighbor and expand its territory both east and west.

Leaving the reader with a total of five alternative "what if?" ideas helps the reader understand that Napoleon's actual decision to sell the Louisiana territory was not inevitable. It was, though, a defining moment—a turning point of enormous impact. In Blumberg's words, "the Louisiana Purchase would *transform* the young United States . . . into a great power respected throughout the world" [emphasis added] (p. 117). While emphasizing the importance of this decision, Blumberg has succeeded in making the reader aware of the competing possibilities. This is a considerable accomplishment.

You can find many more examples in newspapers, magazines, and other biographies and histories. Once I started looking, the examples seemed to pop up everywhere. Finding widespread use of "what if?" demonstrates its usefulness as a way of questioning the past.

More Than Just a Cute Idea

"What if?" is not just another cute idea—something that some writers do to catch their readers' interest. Instead, writers and historians use this technique to explore their own thinking about the past. In the process, they broaden their readers' understanding as well.

Similarly, teaching history is not a question of using cute ideas either. The way we present history has implications for student learning. If we choose to teach history as a predetermined story told by a teacher-storyteller, our students are more likely to see history as a collection of facts bound together in a fixed narrative. But, if we choose to teach history as complex ideas without a predetermined narrative line, students are more likely to see history as an unfinished story that they need to piece together for themselves (Grant, 2001). What we do as teachers counts. "What if?" history is something we can do to question the story line of history. It benefits children in the following ways:

- It highlights the role of decision making in explaining historical events.
- It shows the importance of historical context in understanding history.
- It demonstrates that history is still open to discussion and debate.
- It is an active and engaging way to learn history.

The next chapter, which deals with powerful pairs of biographies, provides another way of establishing history as open to question and interpretation. This chapter focuses on how different authors and illustrators select and shape the facts related to a life story.

Suggested Biographies to Use When Asking "What If?"

Just about any biography can be used when asking *what if.* Here are some suggestions of picture book biographies that would be good choices to begin with.

Adler, D. A. (2000). *America's Champion Swimmer: Gertrude Ederle.* Illustrated by T. Widener. San Diego: Harcourt.
Gertrude Ederle was the first woman to swim the English Channel. She even broke the men's record by almost two hours. But . . . she failed in her first attempt. What if she didn't make a second attempt? What if she listened to the people who thought she couldn't succeed and decided not to try at all?

Bridges, R. (1999). *Through My Eyes.* New York: Scholastic.
Ruby Bridges was the single black child to integrate the William Frantz Elementary School in New Orleans, Louisiana. But . . . what if the NAACP had failed to convince her parents to send her? What if no teacher was willing to accept her as a student?

Brown, D. (2000). *Uncommon Traveler: Mary Kingsley in Africa.* Boston: Houghton Mifflin.
After living at home and hardly ever going outside until she was thirty

years old, Mary Kingsley set off for West Africa in 1893. She had fabulous adventures and saw amazing sights. But . . . what if her dreams took her elsewhere? And what if she didn't return to her home in England?

Carlson, L. (1998). *Boss of the Plains: The Hat That Won the West.* Illustrated H. Meade. New York: DK.
When John Stetson moved to the West during the gold rush days, he applied his hatmaking skills and developed the legendary Stetson hat, called the "boss of the plains." But . . . what if he never went West in the first place?

Cline-Ransome, L. (2000). *Satchel Paige.* Illustrated by J. E. Ransome. New York: Simon & Schuster.
Early in his life, people recognized that Satchel Paige was a gifted baseball player. He played in the Negro major leagues for most of his career, but it wasn't until he was forty-two years old that he was offered a job in the major leagues. But . . . what would his career have been like if he had been offered this job much earlier?

Cooney, B. (1996). *Eleanor.* New York: Viking.
Both of Eleanor Roosevelt's parents died before she was ten years old. She was sent to live with Grandma Hall and later sent to Allenswood school where she developed poise and self confidence. But . . . what if her parents had not died so early? What if she had been sent to live with Uncle Teddy and his family?

Corey, S. (2000). *You Forgot Your Skirt, Amelia Bloomer!* Illustrated by C. McLaren. New York: Scholastic.
Amelia Bloomer went "against the grain" when she refused to act like a proper lady. She supported women's right to vote, started her own newspaper, and refused to wear tight clothing. But . . . did she have to wear *Bloomers*? What if she focused her energies on other issues?

Krull, K. (1996). *Wilma Unlimited.* Illustrated by D. Diaz. San Diego: Harcourt.
Wilma Rudolph overcame polio and went on to become an Olympic star. But . . . what if she didn't push herself so hard? What if her coach hadn't taken such an active role in promoting her career?

Mochizuki, K. (1997). *Passage to Freedom: The Sugihara Story.* Illustrated by D. Lee. New York: Lee & Low.
Chiune Sugihara's decision to disobey his government's orders in order to grant visas to Jews during World War II was a courageous act. Because of his decision, thousands of lives were saved, but he also put himself and his family in danger. What if he had followed his government's advice?

Rockwell, A. (2000). *Only Passing Through: The Story of Sojourner Truth.* Illustrated by R. G. Christie. New York: Knopf.
The slave named Isabella transformed herself into a messenger of the truth, traveling the country to tell of the evils of slavery. She was a free woman, and it was her decision to leave home and become a public figure. What if she had decided to settle comfortably in New York and enjoy her freedom?

3
Powerful Pairs, Triplets, Quads, and More
Looking at Historical Interpretation

P*owerful* pairs, triplets, and quads—for example, two biographies about Louis Armstrong, three biographies about Benjamin Franklin, or four biographies about Eleanor Roosevelt—are just the materials teachers need to help students develop historical literacy. Using these sets is a concrete way to introduce students to the methods historians use to think about their material. I like to think of these sets of biographies as powerful because they enable us to introduce ideas and raise questions about the very essence of history and biography. Using pairs, triplets, and quads, we can ask rigorous questions about how factual material was selected and shaped. Did the biographers:

- use different sources?
- include different information?
- include primary sources?
- provide different versions of past events?
- organize the information differently?
- have different opinions?
- find different meanings or themes in the life story?
- emphasize different ideas?
- discuss their personal connections to the material?
- find different connections between the past and the present?

Historians have a specialized way of reading that involves carefully examining and trying to verify evidence, paying attention to sources, and being mindful of the historical context. This type of reading profoundly affects their writing—yet most students are unaware of this. Instead, students tend to view all reading as the same, whether they are reading science, math, or social studies. One group of adolescents claimed that "they did in history exactly what they did in other courses—used texts, memorized facts, did homework, and took tests" (Bain, 2000, p. 331). Only the facts were different, they felt, not the process of reading. Similar views of reading history exist in the elementary school. Fifth graders who read several sources on the same topic used what researchers called "generic reading strategies they had learned in language arts" (VanSledright & Kelly, 1998, p. 252). One researcher reported that fourth and fifth graders seemed to accept sources uncritically as collections of facts: "Students had no interest in establishing the validity of their information: If they came across information somewhere—anywhere—they included it, and they rarely considered the possibility of looking at more than one source" (Barton, 1997, p. 420). Still other researchers reported that children as young as third graders already had an understanding of "school inquiry," which means "looking it up" and "finding the facts" (Levstik & Smith, 1996, p. 110). Changing this already well-established idea of historical inquiry required persistent effort by the teacher.

When students read history only to collect information, they might just be following their teacher's instructions—doing what they were told to do. As researchers Bruce VanSledright and Christine Kelly reported in their study of a fifth-grade class, "Because the teacher implied that the texts used were sources of uncontested knowledge about the past, students simply mined them for the information they contained" (p. 257). And while reading for information is important, it is only a small portion of what is involved in historical understanding.

If all of this emphasis on fact-finding sounds familiar to you—either because you have been a "fact-finder" yourself or because you still see fact-finding going on in classrooms today, the picture is not as bleak as you might think. Researchers who have interviewed elementary school students see promise in their emerging abilities to evaluate evidence, recognize various points of view, notice differences among sources—in short, to think historically. These researchers suggest that more mature historical thinking can and will develop with instruction that provides:

- "not just time to study *historical content* in depth, but to learn the *language and methods* of historical inquiry" (Levstik & Smith, 1996, p. 110).
- activities which "make visible the 'invisible' cognitive work of historians" (Bain, 2000, p. 333).
- "practice weighing historical evidence, examining biases, syn-

thesizing information and reaching conclusions" (Barton, 1997, p. 426).

- "assistance both in obtaining knowledge of subject matter and in learning to think historically and read critically" (VanSledright & Kelly, 1998, p. 260).

All of this boils down to giving students a different kind of instruction. Instead of presenting all sources as being infallible and indisputable, we can show students how to question what they read. Instead of accepting all sources as being similar and interchangeable, we can look for differences. Instead of assuming that all reading requires the same generic strategies, we can be clear about the specific questions to raise when reading history. With powerful pairs, triplets, and quads, we can look closely at how different biographers write about the same person. We can raise questions about how and why biographies of the same subject can be vastly different. We can show that this is not because one biography is right and all the others are wrong, but because different biographers have selected and shaped the facts they found in different ways. In short, we can show that history involves *interpretation.*

Before discussing specific strategies for using powerful pairs, it is helpful for us to consider what biographers—particularly those who write for elementary and middle school students—have to say about the process of reading for information and then writing biographies. In the discussion that follows I will be referring to articles written by biographers Russell Freedman, Jean Fritz, Milton Meltzer, Jim Murphy, and Diane Stanley. What they say contributes to our understanding of the process of historical interpretation. In fact, these articles, or at least portions of them, would be useful to share with students.

Biography as Interpretation: Listening to Authors

In article after article, biographers tell us that they engage in research, research, and more research. But they do much more. They look for a pattern, a theme, or an organizing principle that makes the facts understandable. In addition, biographers strive to make their books both interesting and informative. They work hard to pique the reader's interest. Creating a coherent, interesting, informative biography requires work—the kind of work students need to know about if they are to develop historical literacy. Yet, traces of this challenging work have been removed from many finished biographies, leaving only well-written narratives. We don't know whether some evidence was discarded because it could not be corroborated. We aren't aware of the process of shaping the narrative and deciding which ideas to highlight and which to downplay or omit. One way to retrieve the biographer's "struggles and strategies along the way" (Bain, p. 333) is to listen to what they have to say about their work. How do they describe what they do? What does writing a biography involve? Understanding the process of writing a biography will help us raise important questions about the resulting works—especially as we look at powerful pairs, triplets, and quads.

Shaping the Structure

Biographers emphasize again and again the role that they play in shaping their material. Here's how Penny Colman, author of numerous history books and biographer of Mother Jones, Madam C. J. Walker, and Fannie Lou Hamer describes this process:

> As I shape the structure, I also search for the essence of the story, the emotional insight, the cognitive concept that I want to illuminate. The search is driven by the sound of my voice in my head repeating, "What's the point, Penny? What's the point? Why are you compiling these facts and true stories?" One of my major points in *Madam C. J. Walker: Building a Business Empire* (1994) was "Madam Walker did much more than make a lot of money" (p. 7). (1999, p. 221)

Other biographers, too, emphasize the active role they play in shaping their material. Milton Meltzer describes the work of the biographer as someone who "makes connections, holds back some of the facts, foreshadows others, decides on juxtapositions, [and] attempts to balance this element against that" (Meltzer, 1989, p. 121). Jean Fritz emphasizes that shaping a biography follows a period of intense research. According to Fritz, "Only after you feel completely at home with the background and circumstances of a life, only after you understand how and why your subject became what he or she became—only then can you sense what your story might turn out to be" (Fritz, 2001, p. 87). Russell Freedman explains that "every time you write a biography or about a historical event, you are rewriting history. There are as many versions of what happened as there are people writing about it. . . ." He concludes, "My books are history according to Russell Freedman" (2002, p. 390).

Clearly, this is much more than fact-finding. Shaping a biography is an active thinking process. As Russell Freedman quipped when asked whether he wrote in longhand, on a typewriter, or on a computer, "You write with your mind. The rest doesn't matter" (quoted in Marcus, 2000, p. 26).

Including Vivid Details and Anecdotes

Biographers talk about searching for "terrific specifics" and anecdotes—those unusual or vivid details and stories that stick in a reader's mind and generate interest. Readers of Russell Freedman's biography of Abraham Lincoln may remember the story of how Lincoln answered the charge of being two-faced by asking, "If I had another face, do you think I'd wear this one?" (Freedman, 1987, p. 1). Readers of Andrea Davis Pinkney's biography of Duke Ellington might recall how young Ellington disdainfully referred to the tunes he was forced to learn on the piano as *umpy-dump* (Pinkney, 1998, unpaged). And, readers of Diane Stanley's *Peter the Great* might remember how Russians who refused Peter's order to cut off their beards had to wear a medal stating that "Beards are a ridiculous ornament" (Stanley, 1986, p. 20). All of us tend to remember and enjoy this type of information.

Because biographers see these details and anecdotes as adding vitality to their work, they are always on the lookout for them. Milton Meltzer describes the search this way:

> The biographer must be constantly sensitive to what he finds that characterizes his subject. Not any fact, but this *particular* fact or phrase or word is what is wanted. Anything that is vivid and human will help the biographer to discover the configurations of a life. (Meltzer, 1989, 334)

Other biographers have made similar comments about the use of vivid detail and anecdote. Diane Stanley (1988) explains how anecdotes can "amuse the readers and act as the glue that holds the rest of the story in their memories" (p. 213). Jean Fritz (1989) reports that "sometimes out-of-the-way details . . . can be depended upon to bring a work to life" (p. 338). And Russell Freedman (1994), well known for his use of anecdote and detail, claims that "a good anecdote can do wonders to reveal character and bring a subject to life" (p. 140).

Vivid details and anecdotes are not the big ideas, generalizations, or major themes involved in biography. Instead, they are bits and pieces of information that contribute to our understanding of the big ideas while, at the same time, keeping us amused and entertained. It is these smaller specifics that make a book lively and interesting, and keep us turning the pages.

Telling the Truth

Biographers are generally adamant about the importance of telling the truth. Despite the growth of "storyographies" (Cummins, 1998)—the mix of fictional story and factual biographical information—writers such as Penny Colman, Russell Freedman, Milton Meltzer, and Diane Stanley emphasize the importance of accurate information. Colman (1999) sums up the truth-telling mandate this way: "Needless to say, I reject the trend in recent years in which some writers add fiction to their nonfiction books in order to move the story along or to make it more dramatic or to introduce facts" (p. 217). Freedman (1994) agrees, stating that while he sees himself as a storyteller, "by storytelling, I do not mean making things up, of course" (p. 138).

It is Freedman who explains the crucial distinction between fiction and nonfiction. According to Freedman, biographers and other nonfiction writers are free to use all the storytelling techniques that fiction writers do, but they must tell the truth. They can describe a setting, develop a character and plot, use flashbacks and flashforwards, and so forth, as long as they do so truthfully. As Freedman says, "I have a pact with the reader to stick to the facts, to be as factually accurate as human frailty will allow" (p. 138).

What these biographers emphasize is that the stylistic techniques that make fiction so appealing are also available to them. In terms of style, fiction and nonfiction are remarkably similar. One critic of children's literature summed up the similarities between fiction and nonfiction this way:

> Writing style in a nonfiction book for children should be, as in all literature, a work of art. Artful prose engages the reader; offers information and enjoyment; is imaginative, accurate, thought provoking, and memorable; and is born of meticulous research. (Jensen, 2001, p. 3)

Truth-telling does not prevent an author from writing artful, well-crafted prose.

Examining Sources

Historians rigorously question their sources, looking for motives and biases, inconsistencies, and just plain inaccuracies. Like a judge or jury, they have to weigh the evidence. Is a source of information consistent with other sources? Would the writer have any reason to bend the truth?

Sometimes biographers find that they cannot entirely trust their sources. Diane Stanley tells us about the problems she found with sources she consulted when working on *Shaka, King of the Zulus* (Stanley &

Vennema, 1988), a biography she wrote in collaboration with Peter Vennema. According to Stanley (1988):

> The primary sources for a life of Shaka are the books written by Henry Francis Fynn and Nathanial Isaacs, Englishmen who spoke Zulu and knew Shaka during his later years. At that time, exotic travel books were quite popular and profitable in England, and Isaacs is known to have written to Fynn suggesting he make his book as sensational as possible to help sales. (p. 216)

She describes another source as being "rich in material, but . . . also the least reliable" (p. 216) since the author had not only invented characters and events, but also had distorted information. She concludes that is it her job as a historian to try to figure out what happened.

When biographers are skeptical about the truth of their sources, they sometimes share their skepticism with readers. Biographers of Mother Jones, the fiery labor organizer, describe how unreliable her writing can be. One biographer wrote that "she [Mother Jones] deliberately misrepresented the facts to gain support for what she thought was right" (Kraft, 1995, p. 3); another wrote that "no one is certain about some facts about Mother Jones" (Josephson, 1997, p. 7).

For students, developing a questioning attitude about sources and even a dose of healthy skepticism adds rigor to reading and research. This is one way we can show students the difference between fact-gathering and historical interpretation. Even when students are reading finished biographies, they can still consider which sources a biographer found credible. If biographers share their thoughts about the sources they used—as James Cross Giblin did in the source notes for *The Amazing Life of Benjamin Franklin* (Giblin, 2000)—they can help students understand the importance of examining sources for bias and accuracy.

Providing Illustrations That Go Beyond the Words

Historical photographs can be an important source of information for biographers. Historian and biographer Jim Murphy told an interviewer, "I really hunt for photographs that don't just reflect what the text is saying, but do even more" (Murphy quoted in Kerper, 2000, p. 121). Murphy reported using a magnifying glass to closely examine photographs in the hope of finding interesting details. Sometimes these details go into his writing; other times they go into captions describing the photographs.

Diane Stanley, who both writes and illustrates her picture book biographies, deliberately adds details in her illustrations that extend the text. She explains, "The pictures go beyond the words, introducing tiny sub-plots which alert children will pick up. These little extras, which all good illustrators use, can also be a teaching device in an historical story" (Stanley, 1988, p. 214).

Biographers understand the importance of photographs and other illustrations as sources of information. Russell Freedman, who pioneered the use of photobiography for children, reports that "for a book with fifty photographs, I might start by collecting three or four hundred" (Freedman quoted in Marcus, 2000, p. 25). Clearly, not any photograph will do.

Students, too, can use photographs to help them understand a historical setting. Since analyzing photographs is a skill that requires instruction and practice (Barton, 2001), examining biographies to see whether the illustrations extend the written text is a useful activity for students.

Using Powerful Pairs, Triplets, and Quads in the Classroom

Using what we know about how biographers interpret factual information, we can raise questions specific to the process of reading and writing history in general and biography in particular. Some of the questions—like those dealing with vivid details and anecdotes—refer to literary criteria. Other questions—like those dealing with selection and interpretation of information—refer to historical thinking. When we show students how to use these questions as a means of considering different biographies of the same person, we are engaging them in the process of historical thinking in a rigorous and discipline-specific way.

Gathering Data Across Biographies

To put a "triplet" to use, I joined a fifth-grade class in the process of considering three different biographies of Benjamin Franklin. These books were:

- *A Picture Book of Benjamin Franklin* (Adler, 1990)
- *What's the Big Idea, Ben Franklin?* (Fritz, 1976)
- *The Amazing Life of Benjamin Franklin* (Giblin, 2000)

While dealing with the same life story and stressing Franklin's many accomplishments, the unique qualities of these books were not missed by the students. The first book is a short, simply written overview of Franklin's career which explores the reasons for considering him a "great

American" (unpaged). In fact, many students thought that because of its simple style the book was more appropriate for younger grades. The second book, while highlighting many of Franklin's "big ideas," is told in author Jean Fritz' characteristic humorous, narrative style. In this book, Fritz makes a number of lists that the students found amusing. For example, she lists some of the streets in Boston in 1706, the year of Franklin's birth: "So far they had Cow Lane, Flownder Lane, Turn Again Alley, Half-Square Court, Pond Street, Sliding Alley, Milk Street, and many others" (p. 7). The third book is the only one that deals with Franklin's difficult relationship with his son William, and the only book to have detailed end notes written by both the author and the illustrator.

My goal was to use these three books to raise questions about historical interpretation. By doing this, the process of historical thinking would become visible and open to discussion. To do this, I used a data chart to collect information about the following issues raised by researchers and biographers:

- accuracy and authenticity
- style
- illustration
- theme
- selection of information
- use of primary sources

In addition, since authors and illustrators sometimes add "notes to the reader" describing their work, I added two other categories—author's note and illustrator's note. A chart like the one in Figure 3–1 was used to gather information across the three books. The questions I used to prompt discussion about these categories are shown in Figure 3–2. These questions helped focus our attention on how history was narrated by the three authors.

After reading and discussing each of the books, the class worked together to complete the data chart. This involved much discussion, and several class periods were devoted to it. Students had their individual copies of the three books, and in the beginning we worked together closely. We considered the first book, *A Picture Book of Ben Franklin,* together and filled in the information about that book. Later, as the children became more comfortable with this process, they were able to work independently on the chart, filling in information about the last book, *The Amazing Life of Benjamin Franklin,* and bringing their notes to a later whole class discussion. Figure 3–3 shows the data chart we completed

FIGURE 3–1 Data Chart for Comparing Powerful Pairs, Triplets, and Quads

DATA CHART: POWERFUL PAIRS

BOOK	ACCURACY AND AUTHENTICITY	STYLE	ILLUSTRATION	THEME	SELECTION AND INTERPRETATION OF INFORMATION	PRIMARY SOURCES	AUTHOR'S NOTE	ILLUSTRATOR'S NOTE

Accuracy
- Is there evidence of the author's research?
- What sources did the author use?
- Did a fact-checker review the manuscript?

Style
- Did the author include vivid details and anecdotes?
- Is the writing imaginative, memorable, and thought-provoking?
- Did the author use different types of sentences and interesting word choices?

Illustration
- Do the illustrations extend the text by providing additional information and interesting details?
- Are captions included that provide additional information and focus the reader's attention on information and details?

Theme
- What is the big idea that is used to organize the facts?

Selection of Information
- What information was included in all of the biographies?
- What information was included in one of the biographies, but not the others?

Primary Sources
- Are primary sources used?
- Is the author convinced that they are reliable? Are we?

Author's Note and End Matter
- Does the author discuss his or her personal interest in the topic?
- Does the author discuss the research process?
- What additional information is provided at the end of the book?

Illustrator's Note
- Does the illustrator discuss the process of creating the illustrations?
- Does the illustrator discuss the research involved?

FIGURE 3–2 Questions for Discussing Powerful Pairs, Triplets, and Quads

together. An examination of the chart shows that students were able to find differences among books in citing sources, style of narration, information contained in illustrations, and so forth. Clearly, they had evidence that one book was not the same as another.

FIGURE 3–3 Data Chart Comparing Three Books About Benjamin Franklin

DATA CHART: POWERFUL PAIRS

BOOK	ACCURACY AND AUTHENTICITY	STYLE	ILLUSTRATION	THEME	SELECTION AND INTERPRETATION OF INFORMATION	PRIMARY SOURCES	AUTHOR'S NOTE	ILLUSTRATOR'S NOTE
A Picture Book of Benjamin Franklin (Adler)	Author didn't list any sources.	Short and choppy sentences. "Ben wrote poetry. He loved books and reading." For beginning readers.	Pictures don't give extra information.	Ben Franklin was a great American.	Most information can be found in any textbook.	None.	Some historians are not sure about the kite-flying story.	None.
What's the Big Idea, Ben Franklin? (Fritz)	No sources listed.	Likes to list things: "Cow Lane, Flownder Lane . . ." Funny: Likes to take facts and point out funny parts.	Pictures gave no extra information. Comical: Funny text with funny drawings. Go well together.	He had <u>many</u> ideas. He had big ideas about daily life, civics, and government.	Not included in any other books: seeing a lion, magic squares, list of street names, being a vegetarian, the electrical picnic.	None.	Notes with extra information, but no note from the author.	None.
The Amazing Life of Benjamin Franklin (Giblin)	Author did list sources. Author traveled to Philadelphia. Two fact-checkers.	Focuses on one topic and then moves on. It's not really funny, though a humorous song is included. Advanced vocabulary.	Pictures tell more than the words. They show people's feelings. Very realistic. Suitable for fifth graders.	Ben Franklin had an amazing life. Called the "wisest American." Tells more about his political life.	Not included in any other books: the arguments between Ben and his son William, falling in love with Madame Helvétius, ballooning, epitaph for his gravestone (B Franklin, printer).	Song Ben wrote. Quote from a letter to his sister.	Discusses primary sources, other books used, and historic sites.	Tells how he did research to make the pictures match Ben's life. Tells how he put in feelings.

Writing About Three Biographies of Ben Franklin

In order to prompt more thinking about the similarities and differences among the books, students were asked to write about one of the categories in the chart (accuracy, style, illustration, etc.) across the three books. To help them organize their writing, I gave them a planning sheet, which asked them to explain their topic, discuss why it was important, and explain the similarities and differences among the three books for just that one topic. So, for example, a student writing about selection and interpretation of information (1) explained the meaning of the topic, (2) compared three books in terms of the information and interpretation offered, and (3) discussed the importance of thinking about this topic. The planning sheet, shown in Figure 3–4, provided students with an organizing frame or support into which they could insert their ideas.

While the students relied heavily on this organizational frame for writing, they seemed to have few difficulties with the assignment. As I examined their papers, what surprised me was the extent to which their comments so closely resembled the thoughts of professional biographers discussed in this chapter, namely, Russell Freedman, Diane Stanley, Penny Colman, and Jim Murphy. It was as if the students picked up on the issues that occupy these biographers and the qualities of writing that they value the most: finding a unique interpretation of the facts, including vivid details and anecdotes, telling the truth, examining sources, and providing illustrations that go beyond the words. A few examples—excerpts drawn from student writing dealing with selection and interpretation of information, illustration, and theme—will illustrate this match.

While considering the impact of the author's choice of what to include in a biography, (see the portion emphasized in bold in Figure 3–5), one student noted that "how an author selects and interprets their [*sic*] information about someone can present a new side of them that readers do not know yet." This comment is reminiscent of Russell Freedman's comments mentioned before, that "every time you write a biography or about a historical event, you are rewriting history. There are as many versions of what happened as there are people writing about it . . ." (Freedman, 2002, p. 390). This student was aware of the creative work of the author.

Another student writing about the illustrations in *The Amazing Life of Benjamin Franklin* (see the portion emphasized in bold in Figure 3–6), commented that "the information that the pictures gave was even more than the words." This reminds me of Diane Stanley's previously quoted comment that "The pictures go beyond the words, introducing tiny sub-

COMPARING BENJAMIN FRANKLIN BIOGRAPHIES: PLANNING SHEET

Topic: ____

Paragraph 1: What is your topic? What does it mean?

Paragraph 2: How are the books similar? (Only in terms of your topic)

Paragraph 3: How are the books different?

Paragraph 4: Why is your topic important?

FIGURE 3–4 Planning Sheet for Comparing Benjamin Franklin Biographies

SELECTION AND INTERPRETATION OF INFORMATION

My topic is selecting and interpreting information. A reader can see what interesting facts and details the author selects to put in the book. Authors also try to anticipate and interpret some of the thoughts and points of view of their subjects.

I think the three books, *A Picture Book of Benjamin Franklin* (Adler), *What's the Big Idea, Ben Franklin?* (Fritz), and *The Amazing Life of Benjamin Franklin* (Giblin), are all very different in how the author selects and interprets information. The first book, *A Picture Book of Ben Franklin,* is just a plain overview of Ben's life. It goes very fast on each topic. There's not much detail or any sense of humor. In the second book, *What's the Big Idea, Ben Franklin?,* there were more details. The author, Jean Fritz, put many facts and details into lists. For example, on page 1, there is a list of street names. On page 21, there's Ben's list of things to do to accomplish more each day. Jean Fritz also interpreted more about his inventions and discoveries. The book was full of humor. The third book, *The Amazing Life of Benjamin Franklin,* focused very deeply on each topic. The book told more about Ben as a politician, like how he helped America become independent. The book was written mostly in a serious way.

Therefore, I think that all three books are very different. **Selection and interpretation of information is important because how an author selects and interprets their [*sic*] information about someone can present a new side of them that readers do not know yet.**

FIGURE 3–5 Student Writing About Selection and Interpretation of Information

plots which alert children will pick up. These little extras, which all good illustrators use, can also be a teaching device in an historical story" (Stanley, 1988, p. 214). In fact, Michael Dooling, the illustrator of the book the student was referring to, noted in an "Author's Note" that "to develop a character or a scene, I like to use the illustration to weave a second emotional line into the story" (Dooling, 2000, p. 46).

Writing about the themes found in the three books, a student commented that "theme is important because the main idea helps you under-

ILLUSTRATION

My topic is illustrations. Illustrations help people express what they want to say in pictures. Illustrations take over your mind and allow you to feel happiness, joy, sadness, and pain. **The illustrations in a book can give you a better understanding of the words.**

In all three books, *A Picture Book of Benjamin Franklin* (Adler), *What's the Big Idea, Ben Franklin?* (Fritz), and *The Amazing Life of Benjamin Franklin* (Giblin), we viewed many illustrations of Ben Franklin when he was young to when he was old. All three books also include illustrations of Ben inventing his wonderful inventions that we can use today.

Each book's illustrations were different for several reasons: style, color and how much information the pictures gave the readers. The first book, *A Picture Book of Benjamin Franklin* has the drawing style of a cartoon. The pictures are extremely colorful and gave less or the same amount of information that the words did. The second book, *What's the Big Idea, Ben Franklin?* has the cartoon style of illustrations. However, the colors were extremely limited and the pictures had the same amount of information that the words did. For example, when Ben Franklin invented the magic math square the book showed a magic math square, plain and simple. The last book, *The Amazing Life of Benjamin Franklin,* had a realistic style. The colors were so expressive and the limit [to the number of colors] was none. Finally, **the information that the pictures gave was even more than the words.** For example, when soldiers were marching to go to war, a little girl is grabbing her mom with a frightened expression on her face.

Illustrations are always important because when you don't understand the words written, pictures guide you and tell you the emotions of the story. The colors set the mood and make you feel happiness, sadness, joy, love, pain, and care. Pictures help you capture the emotions and essence of the book.

FIGURE 3–6 Student Writing About Illustration

THEME

My topic is theme. Theme is the main idea of something. It tells you what the author based the book on and it is usually found at the end of a book. It is there because that is what you should remember about the book.

The theme of all three books, *A Picture Book of Benjamin Franklin* (Adler), *What's the Big Idea, Ben Franklin?* (Fritz), and *The Amazing Life of Benjamin Franklin* (Giblin) was similar because they all thought Benjamin Franklin was an amazing American. They probably thought he was a good role model.

The theme of all three books is different because, even though the authors thought Ben was great, they said it in their own way. The author of *What's the Big Idea, Ben Franklin?* thought he was a great inventor. The author of *The Amazing Life of Benjamin Franklin* thought he took an important part in the Revolutionary War and the writing of the Constitution. The author of *A Picture Book of Benjamin Franklin* just wrote that he was a good American.

Theme is important because the main idea helps you understand the book. **You should know what the author thinks about Ben Franklin and why the author wrote the book.** This is why theme is important.

FIGURE 3–7 Student Writing About Theme

stand the book. You should know what the author thinks about Ben Franklin and why the author wrote the book" (see the portion emphasized in bold in Figure 3–7). This made me think of Penny Colman's self-questioning quoted earlier: "What's the point, Penny? What's the point? Why are you compiling these facts and true stories?" (Colman, 1999, p. 221).

The data chart provided a concrete way of gathering information about the three books, and students were able to build upon it when writing about literary and historical criteria. A look at the three full-length samples (Figures 3–5, 3–6, and 3–7) shows that students noticed many differences among the titles—differences in selection and interpretation of information, illustration, and theme. While the writing is sometimes awkward, the content is perceptive and promising. There is an awareness of the "invisible" decision making involved in writing a biography—decision making that makes each biography unique in some way. Some addition-

ISSUE	STUDENT COMMENT
Accuracy	This shows if the author cited sources, had verification, and whether the book is exact or not. . . . *The Amazing Life of Benjamin Franklin* was very accurate. It listed two fact checkers who checked the book before being published. The author went to Philadelphia to research facts and cited sources in the book's bibliography.
Style	[Style] shows how the author wants to present the book. . . . The two books, *A Picture Book of Benjamin Franklin* and *What's the Big Idea, Ben Franklin?* . . . have choppy sentences. For example, "He was an American hero" (unpaged). *The Amazing Life of Benjamin Franklin* is different because the sentences are longer. For example, "Their conversation turned into a cold hard discussion of family and business matters, and they parted without any show of affection" (p. 36).
Illustration	The books are different because *What's the Big Idea, Ben Franklin?* doesn't give extra information [in the illustration] and pictures are funny. In the book *A Picture Book of Benjamin Franklin* the illustration is colorful but it doesn't give that much information. In the book *The Amazing Life of Benjamin Franklin* the pictures have more information than the other two books and it is colorful. Illustration is important because it might tell more information than the writing.
Theme	Even if they all wrote about Ben Franklin, they had a different point of view. In *The Amazing Life of Benjamin Franklin* the author told us that Ben was a great statesman. *What's the Big Idea, Ben Franklin?* concentrated on Ben Franklin the inventor. *A Picture Book of Benjamin Franklin* wrote about Ben's achievements, but very briefly.

FIGURE 3–8 Student Comments About Issues Raised by Biographers and Researchers

Selection and Interpretation of Information	Only the book *A Picture Book of Benjamin Franklin* talks about how Ben helped set up the first police department. Only the book *What's the Big Idea, Ben Franklin?* talks about how Ben had to pay one penny to see the first lion ever brought to America. [Only] *The Amazing Life of Benjamin Franklin* talks about William Franklin's arguments with his father, how he became the governor of New Jersey, and what happened to him during the Revolution. Some books may not have the same events as another book or talk about the same event/person.
Primary Sources	Primary sources means the quotes in a story. It is something that was written or said which is the exact words of someone. . . . In the book *The Amazing Life of Benjamin Franklin* by James Cross Giblin, the author lists primary sources. He even writes the words of a funny song that the people made up when they were being taxed.
Author's Note	*A Picture Book of Benjamin Franklin* doesn't have a big author's note. It just says that they don't really know if he flew a kite in a thunderstorm. In *What's the Big Idea, Ben Franklin?* the author just lists a little extra information about things in the book, but doesn't tell where the information comes from. In *The Amazing Life of Benjamin Franklin*, the author really tells you where the information comes from.
Illustrator's Note	*The Amazing Life of Benjamin Franklin* is the only book with an illustrator's note. . . .The illustrator's note is important because it tells that the illustrator doesn't guess about the picture and that the illustrator actually took time for the research to draw the pictures. If there was no illustrator's note, people might assume the illustrator just makes up how the pictures are supposed to look.

FIGURE 3–8 *Continued*

al examples of students' comments taken from other essays are shown in Figure 3–8. These comments, too, highlight significant differences among the three books.

Why Bother with Multiple Biographies?

Probably the best answer to "Why bother reading and writing about multiple biographies of the same subject?" is that it is a concrete way of showing history as interpretation. If two, three, or four authors all write biographies of the same person and all are somewhat different, these books provide the basis for learning about multiple perspectives on the past. Powerful pairs, triplets, and quads help us confront the stubbornly persistent belief among students that one source—the RIGHT one—has the truth. One researcher described how fifth-grade "historians" grabbed for an encyclopedia or the fattest book around as THE authoritative answer to their questions instead of seeking out and interrogating other sources:

> "Go to *The* Source," they seemed to be saying. "Why reinvent the wheel?" I was surprised how deeply ingrained this particular position already appeared to be in children who were only 10. (VanSledright, 2002, p. 76)

Instead of a single true source, powerful pairs, triplets, and quads provide us with examples of the multiple possibilities for reconstructing the past. They enable us to see how different biographers select and shape their material. In addition, powerful pairs provide a context for confronting student misunderstandings. Some of my students, for example, assumed that when a book had no bibliography, it was unquestionably inaccurate and not to be trusted. A book without a bibliography was simply "made up" by a lazy author who didn't do any research and could, therefore, be ignored. While bibliographies are essential if students are to see history as constructed, simply having a bibliography doesn't provide a lock on the truth either. Yet this issue would not have surfaced if we had not compared books with and without bibliographies.

Another reason for using multiple biographies of the same subject is that in the process we can introduce students to quality nonfiction literature. There is no better way to learn about shaping and structuring information, using vivid details and anecdotes, examining sources, selecting or creating illustrations, writing captions, and telling the truth than to examine how skillful biographers do it. We are fortunate that so much well-written biography for children is currently available. It is no wonder that "the carpet is usually well worn in the biography section of most public libraries" (Ott, 2002, p. 1281). That's where the good books are. A list of recommended powerful pairs, triplets, and quads that can help you get started on your own study is provided at the end of this chapter.

Finally, there is the added impact of learning historical content. Books about Cleopatra, Joan of Arc, Sojourner Truth, Ernest Shakleton, William Shakespeare, Madam C. J. Walker, Rosa Parks, and others enrich everyone's fund of knowledge and provide interesting material to think about and discuss. One way a number of biographers support the process of dialoguing about the past is by visibly addressing readers—using the words "you," "me," and "I" to create a more personal relationship with the reader. The next chapter shows how this relationship is useful to teachers as a means of promoting dialogue about the past.

Suggested Powerful Pairs, Triplets, and Quads

There are many pairs, triplets, and quads available. The ones listed below include suggestions for picture books and full length biographies. There are, of course, many other possible subjects. Check your library for biographies of people who are particularly interesting to your students or who fit your curriculum needs.

Pairs

MacLeod, E. (1999). *Alexander Graham Bell: An Inventive Life.* Toronto, ON: Kids Can Press. [32 pp.]

Matthews, T. L. (1999). *Always Inventing: A Photobiography of Alexander Graham Bell.* Washington, DC: National Geographic. [64 pp.]

The unique aspects of illustration and format in these two books make for some interesting comparisons. MacLeod's book has a cartoon-like figure of Alexander Graham Bell, referred to in the book as AGB, who speaks directly to the reader. Pointing to a picture of himself as a boy, he states, "That's me at 11. I wasn't a particularly good student" (p. 7). Matthews' book draws heavily on photographs and includes a foreword by Bell's great-grandson.

Fisher, L. E. (1992). *Galileo.* New York: Macmillan. [28 pp.]

Sís, P. (1996). *Starry Messenger.* New York: Farrar Straus Giroux. [32 pp.]

Both Fisher and Sís have distinct artistic styles that would be interesting to examine. In addition, Sís includes numerous excerpts from Galileo's writing, positioned in unique ways. One excerpt, for example, presented in the shape of an eye, gives Galileo's unique view of scientific knowledge.

Aliki. (1999). *William Shakespeare & the Globe*. New York: HarperCollins.
Stanley, D., and P. Vennema. (1992). *Bard of Avon: The Story of William Shakespeare*. Illustrated by D. Stanley. New York: Morrow.
In addition to discussing Shakespeare's life and works, Aliki includes the story of Sam Wanamaker and his efforts to rebuild the Globe. Both books share with readers the gaps in information about Shakespeare's life and how biographers and historians deal with these gaps. Aliki tells readers, "Little is known about him—not even the exact day he was born, or what he looked like" (p. 9). Stanley states that "much of his life is a mystery to us" (unpaged).

Triplets

Adler, D. A. (1989). *A Picture Book of Martin Luther King, Jr.* Illustrated by R. Casilla. New York: Holiday House. [28 pp.]
Bray, R. L. (1995). *Martin Luther King*. Illustrated by M. Zeldis. New York: Greenwillow. [48 pp.]
Rappaport, D. (2001). *Martin's Big Words*. Illustrated by B. Collier. New York: Hyperion. [32 pp.]
One of the most interesting differences among these three books is the use of powerful quotes in *Martin's Big Words*. This attractive book was listed as a "Best Illustrated Children's Book" by the *New York Times* in 2001.

Anholt, L. (1998). *Stone Girl, Bone Girl: The Story of Mary Anning*. Illustrated by S. Moxley. New York: Orchard. [32 pp.]
Atkins, J. (1999). *Mary Anning and the Sea Dragon*. Illustrated by M. Dooling. New York: Farrar Straus Giroux. [32 pp.]
Brown, D. (1999). *Rare Treasure: Mary Anning and Her Remarkable Discoveries*. New York: Houghton Mifflin. [32 pp.]
These three short biographies of fossil hunter Mary Anning differ markedly in their illustrations and writing style. The story is intriguing, but some fictionalized dialogue is found among the books. The lack of a bibliography in any of the books could send students hunting to corroborate information in other sources.

Adler, D. A. (1989). *A Picture Book of Abraham Lincoln*. Illustrated by A. Wallner. New York: Holiday House. [32 pp.]
Cohn. A. L., and S. Schmidt. (2002). *Abraham Lincoln*. Illustrated by D. A. Johnson. New York: Scholastic. [40 pp.]

D'Aulaire, I., and E. D'Aulaire. (1939/1957). *Abraham Lincoln*. New York: Doubleday. [56 pp.]
The older and much more didactic story told by the D'Aulaires contrasts markedly with the newer picture book by Cohn and Schmidt. Consider the D'Aulaire's statement about Lincoln: "He felt like the father of a great flock of children. Some had run away, but were now returning to their home" (unpaged). Now consider the friendlier stance taken by Cohn and Schmidt: "He looks like a giant, doesn't he? He was" (unpaged). The D'Aulaire book is the only one that doesn't mention Lincoln's assassination.

Quads

Dash, J. (2001). *The World at Her Fingertips: The Story of Helen Keller*. New York: Scholastic. [235 pp.]
Lawlor, L. (2001). *Helen Keller: Rebellious Spirit*. New York: Holiday House. [168 pp.]
Nicholson, L. P. (1996). *Helen Keller: Humanitarian*. New York: Chelsea House.
St. George, J. (1992). *Dear Dr. Bell . . . Your Friend, Helen Keller*. New York: Putnam [96 pp.]
Current biographies of Helen Keller seem to stress her social activism. *The World at Her Fingertips* reports her "conversion" to socialism, and *Helen Keller: Rebellious Spirit* contains an epilogue that speculates about what she might have thought about the war in Vietnam, racial turmoil, and the assassination of civil rights activists. *Dear Dr. Bell . . .*, in contrast, focuses on Helen Keller's friendship with Alexander Graham Bell.

Adler, D. A. (1994). *A Picture Book of Sojourner Truth*. Illustrated by G. Griffith. New York: Holiday House. [32 pp.]
Macht, N. L. (1992). *Sojourner Truth: Crusader for Civil Rights*. Philadelphia: Chelsea House. [80 pp.]
McLoone, M. (1997). *Sojourner Truth: A Photo-Illustrated Biography*. Mankato, MN: Bridgestone. [24 pp.]
Rockwell, A. (2000). *Only Passing Through: The Story of Sojourner Truth*. Illustrated by R. Gregory Christie. New York: Knopf. [32 pp.]
R. Gregory Christie's expressive illustrations in *Only Passing Through* make a significant statement about the power of Sojourner Truth. Compare these illustrations with the photographs and paintings in the other books. Also examine the author's note in *Only Passing Through* that explains why the author told the story only up through Sojourner Truth's "transformation."

Adler, D. A. (2001). *B. Franklin, Printer.* New York: Holiday House. [126 pp.]
Adler, D. A. (1990). *A Picture Book of Benjamin Franklin.* Illustrated by J. Wallner & A. Wallner. New York: Holiday House. [32 pp.]
Fritz, J. (1976). *What's the Big Idea, Ben Franklin?* Illustrated by M. Tomes. New York: Coward, McCann & Geoghegan. [48 pp.]
Giblin, J. C. (2000). *The Amazing Life of Benjamin Franklin.* Illustrated by M. Dooling. New York: Scholastic. [48 pp.]

Expand on the work described in this chapter by adding David Adler's recent *B. Franklin, Printer* to your discussion. This longer biography contains many excerpts from primary sources and extensive source notes. Adler is clearly addressing an older, more sophisticated audience than readers of his picture book series.

4
Thinking with Visible Authors

Visible authors speak directly to their readers. Sometimes they reveal their thoughts about the information they have found. Other times, they discuss the process of interpreting this information. Still other times, they challenge readers to interpret the information for themselves. Unlike authors who give us the facts without revealing much about themselves or their thinking, visible authors bring us history with voice, attitude, and point of view. We begin to see the author as intertwined in the telling of the history—visible to us as a thinker, a person with opinions. Most importantly, visible authors establish a friendly bond with the reader—a "you-and-me" connection.

Visible authors reach out to readers, inviting them into a dialogue about the past. They ask, What do you think? In *Phineas Gage: A Gruesome but True Story About Brain Science* (2002), author John Fleischman asks readers to consider the following question: "Was Phineas lucky or unlucky? Once you hear his story, you can decide for yourself" (p. 2). In *A Special Fate: Chiune Sugihara: Hero of the Holocaust* (2000), Alison Leslie Gold asks readers, "Why would a career diplomat act in direct violation of official government policy?" (p. ix). When considering this question she suggests, "If you think that one good person can't morally offset one bad person, then think again" (p. xi). At the end of *You Forgot Your Skirt, Amelia Bloomer!* (2000), author Shana Corey asks, "But did people really forget all about Amelia Bloomer and her improper ideas? Well . . . what do you think?" (unpaged).

Visible authors make it clear that they are interpreters of the facts. Because they share their "take" on information, they give a true picture of what it means to understand history. As one researcher suggested, they "act as a sort of *substitute teacher*, leading students through the primary information, while furnishing clues about the sources of information, its relative importance, degree of certainty, and so on" ([emphasis added] Paxton, 1997, p. 237). And while I would prefer the term "co-teacher" over "substitute teacher," opting for an author to support rather than supplant me in the classroom, the value of visible authors is clear. Students find their writing more interesting, approachable, and informative. One student described it this way: "Someone with like a life wrote it" (Paxton, 1997, p. 242). A friendly, visible author is just the type of person students are willing to interact with while learning the discipline of history.

The idea of paying attention to authors is not new. The book *Questioning the Author* (Beck, McKeown, Hamilton, & Kucan, 1997) presents a rationale and a procedure for helping students to envision and question a sometimes fallible author. The teaching strategy Question-Answer Relationships, or QARs (Raphael, 1986), also focuses students' attention on questions, one of which deals specifically with the author. Students learn that answering one type of question, "author and you," involves combining ideas from both the author and the reader. Similarly, in an article entitled "Reading Authorship into Texts" (Werner, 2000), the writer makes a case for introducing concepts that "make the processes of authorship more visible" (p. 194).

While paying attention to authors is not new, paying attention to visible authors who write about "doing" history and biography is. The immensely important benefit of reading books by visible authors is that they shift our attention to the process of historical interpretation. When visible authors invite us to think with them, they open up the so-called "seamless narrative" of "ironclad history" (Kincheloe, 2001, p. 592) to show the underlying process of sense making. Here's how one researcher summed up the role of visible authors: "The point is that authors wrestle with the credibility of their sources and they puzzle over their interpretations" (Wilson, 2001, p. 254). Because they don't hide this process from us, they show us how to think historically.

Highlighting Historical Thinking: Visible Authors as Teachers

Visible authors who teach about historical thinking write trade books, not textbooks. Unlike these trade books, many textbooks tend to be silent when it comes to historical interpretation. Instead of encouraging dialogue, they encourage passive memorization. Instead of showing how to examine sources and consider historical contexts, they are silent about this process. Because they do not promote dialogue, the relationship between these textbooks and the students who read them has been described as "a deafening silence" (Paxton, 1999, p. 333).

In contrast, visible authors promote conversation by raising discipline-specific questions: Are my sources reliable? Are there gaps in my information? Is it possible to interpret the information another way? Visible authors replace the "deafening silence" with opportunities for a dynamic dialogue. These are opportunities we can build upon in the classroom.

Questioning the Reliability of Sources

Asking questions about sources is one of the most important things historians do. Who is telling me this? What is their motivation? How reliable are they? What if my sources disagree? Then who should I believe? Why?

Visible authors share their questioning stance with readers. They tell us how they deal with sources that might not be entirely trustworthy. In an author's note to *Bull's-Eye: A Photobiography of Annie Oakley* (2001), author Sue Macy tells readers that she encountered many conflicting accounts of Oakley's life. Was she born in 1860, as some claim, or 1866? Where did she first meet her husband Frank, near Cincinnati or Greenville, Ohio? Was her last name spelled Moses or Mozee? Instead of covering up these discrepancies, the author acknowledges, "When conflicting accounts exist, I have consulted a number of different sources and then chosen the alternative that seems most reasonable" (p. 62).

In *Houdini: Master of Illusion* (2001), author Clinton Cox tells us, "There are many stories about how he [Houdini] first became interested in magic" (p. 3). Did he begin as a child who broke into his mother's pie cabinet? Did he work for a professional locksmith when he was just a child? Did the young Houdini work for a traveling circus doing tricks on a trapeze? While dismissing these tales, some told by Houdini himself, Cox tells us that Houdini became interested in magic much later—"probably at 15 or 16, but the exact age is uncertain" (p. 4); and that he "did not learn how to master locks until he was an adult" (p. 3). Cox relates the available stories and then draws his own conclusions, even though when dealing with a subject like Houdini, the author admits that "it's hard to separate fact from fiction" (p. 1).

In the opening pages of Diane Stanley and Peter Vennema's *Cleopatra* (1994), the authors discuss the available sources of information. "Everything we know about Cleopatra was written by her enemies" (unpaged), they tell us. From the start then, we are on the alert that these accounts are not going to present her in a positive light. Then they tell us that other accounts of Cleopatra, those written by Plutarch, were written one hundred years after Cleopatra's death. How accurate can this be? The authors warn us that gossip and propaganda may have influenced this writing. Only after putting us on the alert that even-handed accounts of Cleopatra's life written by her contemporaries are unavailable, do they suggest that there is still much that we do know. This lack of certainty gives readers the feeling—at least it did to me—that the authors carefully weighed the evidence they gathered and reshaped it in a way that seemed most accurate to them. By sharing the process of questioning their sources, Stanley and Veenema—and authors like them—become credible biographers and influential teachers.

Examining the Gaps in Information

One problem that biographers face is the lack of information. What happens when no matter how hard they look for material, they come up empty? No one knows what the subject was doing for several years. There are no records, not even contradictory ones. Instead of the often wished-for smooth, engaging narrative, the story starts and stops abruptly. What a biographer does when this occurs really matters.

In the past, many biographers writing for children felt free to fill in these gaps by creating dialogue and events that seemed plausible, even if they never actually occurred. In fact, many people have fond memories of these books, claiming that fictionalized biographies intrigued them with their stories and generated a later interest in history (Atkins, 2002, p. 31). Unfortunately, while undoubtedly engaging, these fictionalized biographies failed to show how historians deal with gaps in information. This omission has been taken up by current biographers.

Anyone writing about William Shakespeare must deal with the fact that very little is known about his life. Two biographies for children acknowledge this fact. Aliki's *William Shakespeare & the Globe* (1999) and Diane Stanley and Peter Vennema's *Bard of Avon* (1992) both use the word *mystery* to describe Shakespeare's life. From these books readers learn that no one knows precisely when Shakespeare was born, what he looked like, or what his family life was like. Readers also learn another important idea. They learn that when huge gaps like this occur, the biographer has to look for other kinds of information. The authors of these two books examine the times in which Shakespeare lived (the Elizabethan era), his many poems and plays, and the few available personal documents such as his will and other business-related papers. They don't ignore Shakespeare's life, but they make tentative, hedging statements. When Stanley and Vennema speculate about how Shakespeare's life might have been, they sprinkle words like *probably, some people think,* or *we assume* to highlight their uncertainty. Aliki, too, uses *perhaps, no one knows when,* and *some say.* All of this hedging makes it clear that there are gaps and uncertainties in the story of Shakespeare's life.

Walter Dean Myers' *At Her Majesty's Request: An African Princess in Victorian England* (1999) tells how an African princess, saved from death by a British commander, was taken to England where she was protected and guided by Queen Victoria. This is such an unusual story that at the end of the book, the author is still dealing with unanswered questions. In an epilogue, Myers writes "There are . . . so many questions concerning Sarah's life to which I could not find answers" (p. 139). He wonders about how much she remembered about her life in Africa, what she thought about her native country of Dahomey, what she thought about playing with Queen Victoria's children, and more. He even concludes, "It's difficult to sum up her life" (p. 140). This is not a neatly tied package, yet it raises so many interesting questions about war and peace, the meeting of widely differing cultures, and effects of power and weakness, that young readers find it an engrossing tale. Along with the story, they learn how authors deal with gaps in information and nagging questions they cannot answer.

In an author's note to the picture book biography of Madam C. J. Walker, *Vision of Beauty: The Story of Sarah Breedlove Walker* (2000), author Kathryn Lasky boldly states that there are gaps in the story. Yet Lasky reassures readers that she has not fabricated any dialogue. And while the author admits to filling the gaps by "responsibly imagining" (unpaged), she also claims that whenever quotes appear, they are the actual words of Madam Walker. Readers find no fabricated dialogue here.

Offering Alternative Interpretations: Challenging Readers to Think for Themselves

What if the author sees several possible ways to interpret an event or even an entire life story? Possibly, the author is aware that, in addition to his or her own ideas, other biographers have offered a range of interpretations. In this case, the author may choose to let the reader know that this difference of opinion exists.

In *"We Have Conquered Pain": The Discovery of Anesthesia* (1996), author Dennis Brindell Fradin follows the path of four men who claimed to have discovered anesthesia. Fradin reviews the claims of each of the men and their supporters in what he calls "the most bitter medical battle in history" (p. xi). In the end, he concludes that each of the men contributed to the discovery and deserve recognition. Yet, even though Fradin has made up his mind, he tells readers that the controversy still continues. "From time to time we authors revive the controversy . . . , often viewing it in startlingly different ways, depending on our viewpoints" (p. 138).

Fossil Feud: The Rivalry of the First American Dinosaur Hunters (1998) by Thom Holmes is also a story of claims and counter claims. Two scientists who studied dinosaurs, E. D. Cope and O. C. Marsh, maintained an intense rivalry, "always seeking a competitive advantage" (p. 14). Each tried to discover and keep promising excavation sites for themselves, publish new findings about dinosaurs before the other, and assume a leading position in dinosaur science. Near the end of the book, after summarizing the achievements of both men, the author poses the question, "So, what is the answer to the question: Who won the great fossil feud? Cope or Marsh?" (p. 130). After providing sufficient material so that it could be argued either way, he leaves it to the reader to decide.

In the final chapter to *Discovering Christopher Columbus: How History Is Invented* (1991), Kathy Pelta states, "As you begin reading books about Columbus, you may notice that not all authors agree. You must decide which of them to believe" (p. 98). Then she tells how. Readers should track down unusual details to see where they lead. They should examine primary sources. And they should always question everything in terms of its bias and accuracy. In the final chapter entitled "You, the Historian," the author encourages the readers to think for themselves—as historians.

Visible Authors in the Classroom

In this section, I explain how I introduced the work of one visible author to fifth graders and asked them to respond to a challenging question raised by that author. To begin, when dealing with visible authors, it's important to select a well-written book that provides enough information for students to think about and form opinions. This will enable them to respond with conviction.

Selecting a Biography by a Visible Author

Any of the books by visible authors mentioned in this chapter would be good starting points for classroom discussion and writing. I selected *Joan of Arc* (1998) by Diane Stanley because—in addition to the way the author speaks directly to the reader—this biography is an outstanding piece of literature to use in the middle grades.

Since the story of Joan of Arc is likely to be unfamiliar to many youngsters, the author provides necessary background information. She begins the book with a discussion of the setting, war-torn France, explaining that the Hundred Years' War is raging and destruction is all around. The English king has claimed that the French throne belongs to him, and as a result, the two countries are at war. The French Duke of Burgundy and even the French queen support the English. Only the crown prince Charles VII, known as the Dauphin, stands in the way of a takeover. Into this setting the author introduces Joan—an illiterate peasant girl who will intervene to prevent the English domination of France. She is a most unlikely figure to change the course of events.

In addition to explaining the historical context, this biography is clearly written and beautifully illustrated by the author. The illustrations provide additional information about the setting. An opening picture of the house Joan lived in with her family shows her at work spinning, seated next to a churn in a room with a dirt floor. A woman, probably her mother, is sweeping the floor, and a young man, probably her brother, is carrying in wood. Everyone is wearing clothing with patches. A large cross—a sign of the family's religious convictions—is on the wall. While the written words tell us that Joan was poor, the illustration shows what this poverty looked liked.

The book follows the course of Joan's life in chronological order. It begins when Joan first sees visions and hears voices telling her that she must escort Charles, the crown prince, to the cathedral at Reims where he will be crowned king—a feat which she accomplishes. It ends with a discussion of the events following Joan's capture, trial, and conviction by a court of the Inquisition, and her death. Twenty-five years after her conviction, there was an effort to have her declared innocent of the charges brought against her and this effort succeeded.

In the final two paragraphs of the book, the author steps aside from the chronological story, providing the springboard I needed to discuss historical interpretation. In the next to last paragraph, the author establishes the credibility of her sources. She refers to the transcript of Joan's trial as *autobiography*, since during that ordeal Joan discussed her life in her own words. She refers to the transcript of her Trial of Rehabilitation as Joan's *biography*, since it included testimony of people who knew her. These sources, according to the author, are credible, yet what do they mean?

In the last paragraph—a stunning finish to this book and a real find for teachers—the author asks this question: *"But now that we have the story, what are we to make of it?"* (emphasis added, unpaged). She then offers three possible interpretations:

1. *The visions and voices were real.* Joan was visited by saints who told her what she must do.
2. *The visions and voices were hallucinations.* They were probably the result of some undetermined illness.
3. *The visions and voices were wishful thinking.* Joan knew of a prophecy that a young girl was destined to save France and hoped that she was that girl. Ultimately, this hope changed into a firm conviction that, indeed, she was that girl.

Since no one can really know for sure what to make of the visions and voices, here is an opening for students to explore. The heartening result I found is that with a little bit of support, fifth-grade students jumped at the chance to express their opinions.

Answering a Question Posed by a Visible Author

After reading and discussing *Joan of Arc*—a process which took a considerable amount of time given the vocabulary, the names of people and places, and the ideas encountered in the book—students were ready to tackle the big question.

To support their efforts to respond, I provided them with a planning sheet (see Figure 4–1). While this sheet specifically focused on the question raised by Diane Stanley, other similar sheets can be constructed for questions raised by other authors. This particular planning sheet guided students to go back to the book to re-examine Joan's claim about visions and voices, and then to decide *what* they thought about this claim and *why*. It helped students by providing a way to gather evidence to support their theories. While it did result in a similar three paragraph structure for most of the writing, the content of this writing was remarkably dissimilar. With continued practice writing about questions such as this one, there should be less need for these teacher-prepared planning sheets and, as a result, more flexibility the way students respond.

JOAN OF ARC

Writing: How do I make sense of the miraculous visions and voices?

Ask yourself: What do I make of it?

Paragraph 1: *Visions and Voices:* Explain Joan's claim about visions and voices. Go back to the book to look over the information.

Paragraph 2: *What I Think:* Explain your theory.

Paragraph 3: *Reasons for My Theory:* Explain why you believe your theory is right. Use words like *first, second,* and *third* as you list and explain each reason.

FIGURE 4–1 Planning Sheet for Responding to a Visible Author

Students took each of the three possible positions outlined by Diane Stanley and offered a range of reasons why. A look at several writing samples will give you an idea of their thinking.

Arguing that the visions and voices were real. Most students seemed convinced that the visions and voices were divine revelations. Several of these responses began by giving reasons for dismissing the other two interpretations. They asked questions such as, "How could hallucinations provide information about the Hundred Years' War?" or "How could hallucinations make predictions that ended up being true?" One student even argued that the Saints gave Joan a miraculous boost in confidence and understanding, enabling her to speak brilliantly at her trial. She was, in effect, transformed by her interaction with the Saints. As part of this student's argument, he wrote:

> I also think Joan really saw the Saints because when she was on trial, she gave clever answers and was acting smart even though she was an uneducated peasant. That kind of made me think that the Saints weren't going to let Joan give up. They helped Joan change.

All writers launched into a listing of their many reasons, noting that at every turn she seemed to know the right answers. Prompted by the planning sheet to make a list of reasons for their theory, they did so. Many noted, for example, that when Joan identified Charles, the dauphin, in a crowded room of people, he tried to trick her by saying he was not the prince. Yet Joan stood firm. Another frequently recalled reason was that Joan predicted that she was going to be wounded in battle and she was. As you can see by examining last paragraph of the writing sample in Figure 4–2, the list of reasons was often lengthy. Such a record of accomplishments, according to this writer and others, doesn't happen by chance.

Arguing that the visions and voices were hallucinations. Those students who argued that the visions and voices were hallucinations generally claimed that they had to be false because they had failed to protect Joan from a horrible death (see Figure 4–3). In effect, they had left her in the lurch. Others argued that it wasn't normal to jump from a 60- or 70-foot tower the way Joan did when she tried to escape from prison by killing herself. Another student said that a "normal" girl back then would not have cut her hair the way Joan did. Still another claimed that Joan's visions and voices were caused by the unsanitary environment in which she was living. One student wrote:

Joan claimed while she was feeding the birds, she heard a voice. When she turned around she saw a glorious light. The third time she heard the voice, she saw a vision of Saint Michael. Later, she saw visions of Saint Margaret and Saint Catherine. They had told her to be a good and pious girl and go to church often. Every time they left she cried. But when they came back, her heart was full of joy. The more they came, the sadder the news they told her. They told her about the Hundred Years' War, and how much help the French needed to win a great victory. They told her that she was to lead the French to victory, even though she was a small girl. Joan was stunned by the news, but if God told her to do this she would do it. She tried to get started on the mission right away.

My opinion is that the visions and voices were exactly what she said they were: divine revelations. If she was sick in the body or mind, she would have seen other visions, too. She was very pious so, out of the whole country, if God did ask someone to lead the French to victory, it should have been her. If these were hallucinations, they wouldn't have known about the Hundred Years' War and all those predictions that were right, weren't just coincidences. If she had heard about the rumor of a lady losing France and a virgin about to save France, and wished it was her so much that she started believing it was her, it doesn't explain the visions, voices, or glorious light. Nobody is sure of the real reason she saw the visions and voices so I have 1/3 chance of being right.

I have some reasons to support my theory. First, her prediction was right about the French losing the Battle of Orleans. Second, she found the real Charles when he said he wasn't and tried to trick her. Third, while she was taking a nap, she had a dream that the French were losing a battle real badly, and she was right. Fourth, when a guard had insulted her with a crude remark, she said, "You're so near your death," and later that day he died by falling in a moat. Fifth, when she jumped off the tower when she was held prisoner by the Burgundians, a guard had found her and there was not a scratch in sight. People die jumping from that height. Sixth, she told him [the guard] a sign and somehow he believed she was from God. Seventh, she knew the exact place (above the chest) she was to be wounded in a battle that was about to be held. Finally, [earlier] when the priests tested her to make sure that she was from God and not the devil, she was proved to be from God.

FIGURE 4–2 A Student Arguing That the Visions and Voices Were Real

When Joan was working alone in the garden, the church bells began to ring. Suddenly, she heard voices. Turning to see who it was, she only saw a brilliant light. She didn't tell anyone about the voices and soon it came again. The voices told Joan to go to the town of Vaucouleurs to ask for an armed escort to protect her on the journey to Chinon.

I really think that Joan's visions and voices were actually hallucinations produced by some illness of the mind and body. Since she was illiterate and uneducated, she would probably believe anything people would tell her. That is why in the first place she had those visions and voices. She probably made them up in her head or it was just her imagination.

I believe my theory is correct because first of all, when Joan was on trial, that's when she needed the visions and voices the most, and they weren't there for her. That was the only thing that gave her confidence. Secondly, if the voices had come, they would have told her how to protect herself and she probably wouldn't be burned to death! But they didn't come at all! If they came for Joan they would've helped her out. Thirdly, the visions said that she would be saved from the English, but she wasn't. They lied to her. That is why I believe the theory that she was hallucinating because she was sick of mind and/or body.

FIGURE 4–3 A Student Argues That the Visions and Voices Were Hallucinations

> Since she wasn't very clean, she could have become sick with high fever and seen her visions. First, Diane Stanley mentions in her book that no one in Joan's village was likely to be clean. For example, Joan's house had dirt floors and there were no bathrooms in her village. Second, since the village wasn't clean, the animals that lived there could have gotten sick and then they could have spread a disease that made Joan see and hear things that weren't even real. Third, since the village was burned by the English, the smoke could of caused some damage to the brain. The damage might have caused her to believe the Saints were real and could talk to her.

In short, a considerable number of children argued that Joan, for one reason or another, was ill and that the visions and voices could best be explained by hallucinations. But this last explanation about the lack of cleanliness reminds me of our not so distant concerns about mad cow disease, viruses, and wildfires. We always, in effect, tell about ourselves and our concerns when writing history.

Arguing that the visions and voices were wishful thinking. Only one student argued that the visions and voices were wishful thinking. This student refused to believe that Joan had any mental problems and suggested, instead, that she made her claims on purpose because she felt people would believe her. As Figure 4–4 shows, according to this argument, a desperate Joan—a girl who never really saw any visions or heard any voices—acted deliberately to do what had to be done. After all, this writer argues, visions "don't just pop up in your face." Instead, an intelligent Joan conned people who were "so desperate they would believe anything without much reasoning." This is no ignorant peasant girl.

As I look back on this work, I am impressed with the ability of fifth graders to respond to a question raised by an author. And it is not just any question; it is a lingering question still pondered by historians and others intrigued by this particular story. I am impressed and I am reminded of what I already know—that students do not just "take in" historical information we place before them. They think about it, evaluate it, and respond to it. Students are not natural memorizers. They are, instead, natural interpreters.

Why Bother to Dialogue with Visible Authors?

It's always possible to read books like *Joan of Arc* or other biographies mentioned in this chapter and never take the time to really think about the questions that authors are raising, or to ask our students to think about them. In doing so, we might gain a great deal of factual information, but we wouldn't be learning much about history. History always involves asking questions and answering them for ourselves. It's a process, not a product. Since, as I've said before, it's a time-consuming process, I'll offer what I see as the continuing benefits for doing it anyway. In this instance, I'll focus on the benefits of learning the process of historical thinking from visible authors.

First, the questions raised by visible authors are still open to interpretation. They are not test questions or questions whose answers can be found within the pages of the book if you only look hard enough. They

HOW I MAKE SENSE OF THE MIRACULOUS VISIONS AND VOICES

When Joan was thirteen years old, [she said] she started to hear and see visions and voices. These visions told her to be a good little girl, go to church often, and about the terror in France. Joan loved seeing these visions very much. These visions were of some Saints that died a long time ago. She was religious and was glad that they came to her. Every time they left, Joan would cry.

I don't think Joan really saw these visions. She was probably imagining them or saw them through a dream. She felt that her country's people were dying and needed help. Joan was desperate to save France. She might have used the story about the Saints as an excuse to help her along the way. When she heard of the prophecy of "The Maid," she thought she was the chosen one.

There are a few reasons why I believe Joan was imagining these visions and voices. First, it is impossible for visions to pop up in front of your face. Strange noises or voices aren't possible either. This never happened to anybody that I know of. Second, Joan was very religious, and back then, people believed in monsters and ghosts. So, Joan could tell everyone that she was the 'Miraculous Maid' and most of the people would believe her. Because they were so desperate, they would believe anything without much reasoning. Third, Joan doesn't seem to have any mental problems. She tried to save France because the thought it was her duty. Even though she was a peasant girl, she was smart and died for her country.

FIGURE 4–4 A Student Argues That the Visions and Voices Were Wishful Thinking

are, instead, questions that people are still debating: "Who do you think is right? Who would you believe? What do you think might have happened? What do you think all this means? What do these facts add up to?" These are questions historians are attempting to answer now and will continue to attempt in the future. In answering questions posed by visible authors, students are engaging in an authentic process. They are seeing first-hand that instead of a set of facts to learn, history is "an ongoing conversation and debate"—"a place to invent'" (Holt, 1990, p. 13).

Second, this is an invitation that is too good to pass up. Speaking as a busy teacher, I welcome the assistance of an author as a co-teacher. Several years ago, I realized that authors of well-written history books could help me shape my teaching. I was reading James Giblin's book *When Plague Strikes: The Black Death, Smallpox, AIDS* (1995), when I came across the following generalization about the three epidemics: "All three have had disastrous impacts on the affected populations and left lasting social, political, religious, and cultural consequences in their wake. As each of the diseases has run its deadly course, people reacted in similar ways" (p. 7). I wondered, was Giblin right? To test this out, I immediately constructed a chart for each plague listing the categories: (1) people's immediate reaction, (2) impact on the population, and (3) lasting consequences. These charts helped me as I worked with sixth graders to test out Giblin's generalization and to make comparisons among the three plagues. I concluded then that "thinking alongside the author" was a powerful thing to do because it enabled students "to examine and discuss the data offered, and then to extend the conversation by including their own thoughts on the topic" (Zarnowski, 1997, pp. 11–12; see also Zarnowski, in press). The possibilities for powerful teaching that Giblin's book opened up to me are available in many other books as well. It's simply a question of looking for the openings that visible authors are providing us and then using them to support and enhance our teaching.

Third, there is no need to wait to ask elementary and middle school students to interpret history. Their enthusiasm for this activity is remarkable. Not one child who was asked to answer Diane Stanley's question about visions and voices responded with "I dunno" or "Don't ask me!" or "How am I supposed to know?" On the contrary, they plunged right in. And just in case you think that I was working with a select group of gifted students whose work is beyond the reach of most kids—a common response to some of the samples I have collected—let me assure you that the students I worked with are in a "regular" New York City public school.

Nor am I the only person with such faith in students' ability to think for themselves. In his book about teaching social studies, *Getting Beyond the Facts*, Joe Kincheloe advocates the use of divergent questions when teaching history. He says that "students operating in the cognitive conventions of everyday life seem to think on a higher level than that of traditional schooling" (p. 595). In other words, they are already comfortable thinking for themselves.

Fourth, it is worth repeating that students who come up with original interpretations of the past develop a truer sense of history. This is important because so many of us learned about the process of doing history after we became adults. Just this week I came across the following remark by a Yale Ph.D. in history who is also the author of an outstanding children's history book: "I was in college before I realized that historians disagree with each other about many aspects of our country's past" (Seidman, 2002, p. 37). Strategies like responding to visible authors bring various viewpoints out in the open so that children grow up knowing that history is a vibrant subject still open to dialogue and debate.

Besides dialoguing with visible authors, there are other ways of engaging youngsters in molding and remolding historical information. The next chapter deals with enhancing a historical narrative by adding to it through the use of sidebars, author's notes, and illustrated timelines. These features not only have an impact on how history is told, they also affect how it is read.

Suggested Biographies to Use When Seeking a Visible Author

Many of my favorite books with visible authors were already mentioned in the chapter, but here are some additional recommended titles. These books make excellent starting points for discussion and writing about sources, gaps in information, and multiple interpretations. There are, of course, many other biographies you can use. Once you begin to look for visible authors, you can easily spot them.

Reliability of Sources

Greenfeld, H. (2001). *After the Holocaust.* New York: Greenwillow. [146 pp.]

In a preface to this collective biography of the lives of eight Holocaust survivors during the period following World War II, the author alerts us to the fact that people remembering painful events have selective memories. He tells us, for example, that many of his subjects remember the camps for displaced persons fondly; in reality, many camp members staged protests. He reminds us that oral histories can contain small inaccuracies, even when given by people directly involved in historical events. This in no way detracts from the powerful stories in this book. While reading the various histories, students might wonder about which information might be open to question, and which is definitely not.

Meltzer, M. (1997). *The Many Lives of Andrew Carnegie.* Danbury, CT: Watts. [160 pp.]
A note a man writes to himself might seem like a reliable source of information. Yet, as this biography beautifully illustrates, that's not always the case. In a chapter entitled "A Memo to Himself," the author discusses how Carnegie at age thirty-three wrote a note vowing to quit his business enterprises in two years and devote himself to self-improvement and civic pursuits. Did he do this? Not until thirty-three years later! This chapter is a wonderful example of how authors make sense of their sources. In fact, the idea that Carnegie was a conflicted person—a man who loved amassing great wealth but who also was repulsed by it—dominates this book.

Reich, S. (1999). *Clara Schumann: Piano Virtuoso.* New York: Clarion. [118 pp.]
This well-documented biography, full of photographs and excerpts from primary sources, also deals with the question of sources. In an epilogue entitled "Pieces of a Puzzle," the author deals with the many sources of information available to biographers. But, just in case you think writing about Schumann is a straightforward affair, she tells us that for years Clara Schumann's father wrote in her diary, pretending to be her. This epilogue is a wonderful starting point for talking about the differences among sources and how—to use the author's words—biographers use different sources to put "the pieces of the puzzle" together.

Gaps in Information

Adronik, C. M. (2001). *Hatshepsut: His Majesty, Herself.* Illustrated by J. D. Fiedler. New York: Atheneum. [40 pp.]
Despite the attempts of her successor, Tuthmosis III, to erase all evidence of Hatshepsut's reign as the first successful female pharaoh, some evidence did emerge and more continues to emerge. By explaining how this story only gradually came to light, the author shows readers that sometimes gaps in historical information do get filled in . . . at least partially. The author concludes that we may never know the full story. This book should prompt discussions about how history continues to be researched and rewritten—even ancient history.

Lasky, K. (1994). *The Librarian Who Measured the Earth.* Illustrated by K. Hawkes. Boston: Little, Brown. [48 pp.]
In an author's note, Katherine Lasky discusses how she became interested in Eratosthenes, the Greek librarian who determined the circumference

of the earth. Lasky also reveals the gaps in information about his personal life and comments on the necessity to look at the times in which he lived. Lasky concludes that she cannot create facts, but that she can only imagine what his life was like. This book provides an excellent starting place for discussing gaps in information and how authors handle them. Compare the author's note in this book with authors' notes by Diane Stanley and Peter Vennema in *Bard of Avon* and Aliki in *William Shakespeare & the Globe* to see how other authors deal with subjects whose personal life is a mystery.

Levinson, N. S. (1990). *Christopher Columbus: Voyager to the Unknown.* New York: Dutton. [118 pp.]
This book begins with an author's note that raises many unresolved questions about Columbus and alerts readers to the continuing debates among historians. Even today scholars argue about exactly where Columbus first landed, whether he was the first aboard ship to site land, and whether he was a genius or a self-serving seeker of fortune. The author's statement at the beginning of the book that "different viewpoints and new evidence are frequently what make history exciting to scholars (p. viii)" could set students off on an inquiry about how various biographers portray Columbus and how they deal with the gaps in information.

Multiple Interpretations

Yolen, J. & H. E. Y. Stemple. (2001). *The Wolf Girls: An Unsolved Mystery from History.* Illustrated by R. Roth. New York: Simon & Schuster. [32 pp.]
———. (1999). *The Mary Celeste: An Unsolved Mystery from History.* Illustrated by R. Roth. New York: Simon & Schuster. [32 pp.]
Though not biographies but histories, these books in "The Unsolved Mystery from History" series provide excellent starting points for discussing multiple interpretations. In *The Mary Celeste,* the authors provide six theories of what happened to a ship found afloat without its crew and challenge readers to come up with their own theories. In *The Wolf Girls,* readers are challenged to figure out whether two girls brought to an orphanage in India had been, as some claimed, raised by wolves. Four different theories are provided and readers are encouraged to come to their own conclusions.

Freedman, R. (1999). *Babe Didrikson Zaharias: The Making of a Champion.* New York: Clarion.
In one of the most interesting "multiple" interpretations I have ever found, author Russell Freedman discusses how this book about Babe Didrikson

Zaharias was written nearly four decades after he first wrote about her in *Teenagers Who Made History* (Holiday, 1961). In revisiting this subject, he made new discoveries. This is a wonderful example of re-seeing and reinterpreting.

5
Sidebars, Captions, Timelines, and Authors' Notes

What else can I include? In addition to the life story, some biographers seem to be asking themselves, "What else? Is there more?" Is there information that is interesting, but might be tossed aside because it's too detailed? Perhaps it's like an aside or a "by the way." It's information that takes the main story off on a detour. It could be additional thoughts about how the author first became interested in the subject. The biographer shares the answer to the question, "Why did I select this particular subject? What made this life story interesting to me?" Sidebars, captions, timelines, and author's notes provide opportunities for writers to add this "what else?" information to a biography.

Features like sidebars and other innovative graphics are changing the look of current biographies and the way we read them. These features are part of what author Eliza Dresang calls a "radical change" in book design that has emerged from computer technology, Internet websites, and CD-ROMS (Dresang, 1999; Dresang & McClelland, 1999). These features are noticeable in some biographies for young readers. Among the emerging formats are:

- Graphics in new forms and formats. Words may vary in color, size, and font and placement on the page. They may be superimposed on or around pictures.
- Nonlinear organization. Information may be given that is not in sequential order. It is up to the reader to make connections among various bits of information offered.
- Synergy, or a strong melding, between words and pictures. Both work together to provide information. One doesn't embellish the other.

"Radical change" features make books more interactive and provide greater access to information. Sidebars and related graphics, captions, timelines, and author's notes provide readers with options. A reader can approach a book by examining the pictures first, by reading the sidebars, or by sampling a bit of each—all of this before even beginning the main text. There is no need to always read in a linear way from the front to the back of a book. In fact, I usually head for the back of a biography first, looking for the sources, and then I check for an author's note. Once I get a sense of who is writing the biography and the research that underlies it, I am ready to consider what the author has to say. This opportunity to pick and choose among the access features that provide multiple ways into a book allows readers to "flip back and forth," building meaning as they go (Kerper, 2002).

Similarly, writers using sidebars, captions, timelines, and author's notes as they construct a biography have multiple options for presenting information to readers. What are the major events that belong in the main text? What can be placed in a sidebar off to the side of the main text? Would a photograph or an illustration present information about historical context better than a written description? Should a caption be used to highlight visual information or point out something that shouldn't be missed? Should a personal connection to the subject be placed in an author's note? Could additional information, besides a list of dates and events, be placed in a timeline? Access features allow biographers some flexibility in shaping their material.

I do not want to give the impression that a radical shift is rocking the genre of biography. Instead, I want to highlight some options that make the reading and writing of biography more flexible and, in my opinion, more interesting. In this chapter I will show how easily youngsters incorporated these features into their writing. All it took was a brief introduction to biographies using "radical change" or "what else?" features and a process for sustained reading and writing.

Updating the Snapshot Approach to Biography

For students to enhance biography with sidebars and other features, they have to be engaged in the process of reading and writing original biographies. Then the sidebars, captions, timelines, and author's notes they create can become integral parts of the biography, not extra ornaments. To get started on this, I worked with a class of fifth graders and their teacher to begin writing what would become an updated version of "snapshot biographies" (Zarnowski, 1990).

This approach, which I described more than ten years ago, challenges children to research and shape original biographies of historical figures. They select the events they consider important enough to draw and write about. By doing this, they bring order and meaning to the material they uncover. There are four basic steps to the process: (1) learning about the subject by reading, researching, and responding to information in journals, (2) brainstorming a list of remembered events and selecting the most significant events to write about and illustrate, (3) preparing the "snapshots"—illustrations and written descriptions of the selected events—and (4) arranging the snapshots in chronological order and writing a summary statement that highlights the main idea of the biography.

This has proven to be a simple and serviceable approach for getting even young children into "doing biography." Student teachers and undergrads in my college classes have successfully used this approach with children. Because I, too, have been through the process many times, I felt eager to enhance it with newer access features.

To begin, the class was divided into two groups. One group researched the life of Sir Ernest Shackleton, the explorer whose attempt to cross Antarctica is one of the greatest survival stories ever. The other group researched the life of Amelia Earhart, the famous pilot whose mysterious disappearance during her attempt to fly around the world is still being questioned. These two historical figures were selected for two reasons. First, because they are both widely written about, students would have no trouble finding information to put into sidebars, captions, or timelines. Second, because both figures tested the limits of what was considered possible—Shackleton in terms of human endurance and Earhart in terms of what women could accomplish. I thought students would find their life stories interesting.

Each group began by reading a book in the National Geographic photobiography series—either *Trial by Ice: A Photobiography of Sir Ernest Shackleton* (Kostyal, 1999) or *Sky Pioneer: A Photobiography of Amelia Earhart* (Szabo, 1997). This highly visual series, which draws from the resources of the National Geographic Society, was an excellent starting point for a project that would involve both writing and illustrating. As the students completed these books, they moved on to other resources, and began thinking about writing their own biographies of either Shackleton or Earhart. At that point, I introduced the "what else?" features that would update the snapshot biography and bring it into the twenty-first century.

Using a Teacher's Eye to Examine Literature for "What Else?" Features

Finding the right children's literature to use as examples of "what else?" features was essential. Like many other teachers, I selected literature with an eye toward both appreciation and utility. First, I was concerned with the sheer enjoyment of introducing interesting books to children. I have often heard teachers make comments like, "I know the kids will love this!" This is an important concern when sharing history and biography. We need to identify material that students find appealing—material with the "magical power" (Freedman, 2000, p. 19) of history and biography.

But I needed more. In addition to fostering literary appreciation, I needed material that would help me teach about history and biography—books that would "provide exciting possibilities to understand the past and for further developing students' historical consciousness" (Trofanenko, 2002). Books like the ones discussed next can do this because they show the many possibilities for presenting historical information. They definitely opened up intriguing options for the students I worked with as they wrote about Amelia Earhart and Sir Ernest Shackleton.

Sidebars and Other Interesting Graphics

The first feature I discussed with the students was sidebars, columns of additional information along the side of the page. Three examples from picture book biographies show some of the ways biographers use sidebars—to add information, to define words, and to provide quotations. In *Snowflake Bentley* (Martin, 1998), a biography that chronicles Wilson Bentley's growing interest in studying snowflakes and his determination to learn how to photograph them, sidebars add extra information. The opening page of the main text describes the setting as a time "when farmers worked with ox and sled" (unpaged), while a sidebar that follows gives the exact time and place of Bentley's birth—February 9, 1865 in Jericho, Vermont. This information gives a more specific context to the story. In *Handel, Who Knew What He Liked* (Anderson, 2001), sidebars help readers by defining words used in the main text. The book begins by telling how young Handel smuggled a clavichord into the house and up the stairs without his parents' knowledge, while a sidebar on the same page tells what a clavichord is, how it works, and how it differs from a piano and a harpsichord. In *Starry Messenger* (Sís, 1996), the biography of Galileo Galilei, the sidebars feature a number of quotations from Galileo's writing. On one page, for example, the main text simply relates Galileo's amazement at what he saw through his telescope, while a sidebar gives four quotes in which Galileo describes his observations of sunspots. Sidebars like these can boost our background knowledge by explaining the historical context and defining unfamiliar words. In addition, they can extend what we already know by giving us additional information.

Interesting graphics communicate information and emphasize ideas, too. In *Martin's Big Words* (Rappaport, 2001), the main text on almost every page is followed by a quote from Martin Luther King written in bold, colorful type. By the last page of the book, King's words clearly dominate the main text which consists of only a single sentence. The power of Martin's words *is* the message. His words stand out because they are bigger, more colorful, and more powerful than the text. In *Woody Guthrie: Poet of the People* (Christensen, 2001), the words to "This Land Is Your Land," probably Guthrie's most famous song, are printed in big, bold letters across the top of each page. While the main text describes Guthrie's travels across this country, the bold print shows how this song incorporates what he saw. In *Alexander Graham Bell: An Inventive Life* (MacLeod, 1999), a handsome full-page collage combining photographs, primary source documents, and a caricature of Bell who speaks directly to the reader using comic book–style speech balloons complements each written page, providing additional information and adding visual interest. This format challenges the reader to connect the various pieces with the main narrative.

While the books mentioned here are generally available in public libraries, they are only meant to suggest examples of books that can be used to show students how information can be presented in a biography using sidebars and graphics. In each case, the sidebars and graphics work to explain and extend the information in the main text.

The fifth graders I worked with easily incorporated sidebars and graphics into their biographies of Shackleton and Earhart. Like the authors of the picture book biographies just discussed, they were able to explain and extend the information in the main text. Figures 5–1a and 5–1b show how a sidebar extends information in the main text by discussing what early pilots wore; this sidebar is part of a more comprehensive, two-page presentation that includes text, illustrations, and captions. Figure 5–2 adds "Did you know?" or extra information about Shackleton's expedition. Here the facts range from topic to topic, including scurvy, penguins, desert geography, and living in an overturned boat. Using the information provided in the rest of the biography, the reader must make the connections among these facts. In Figure 5–3, the sidebar moves away from the side

FIGURE 5–1A Amelia Earhart Biography with Sidebar

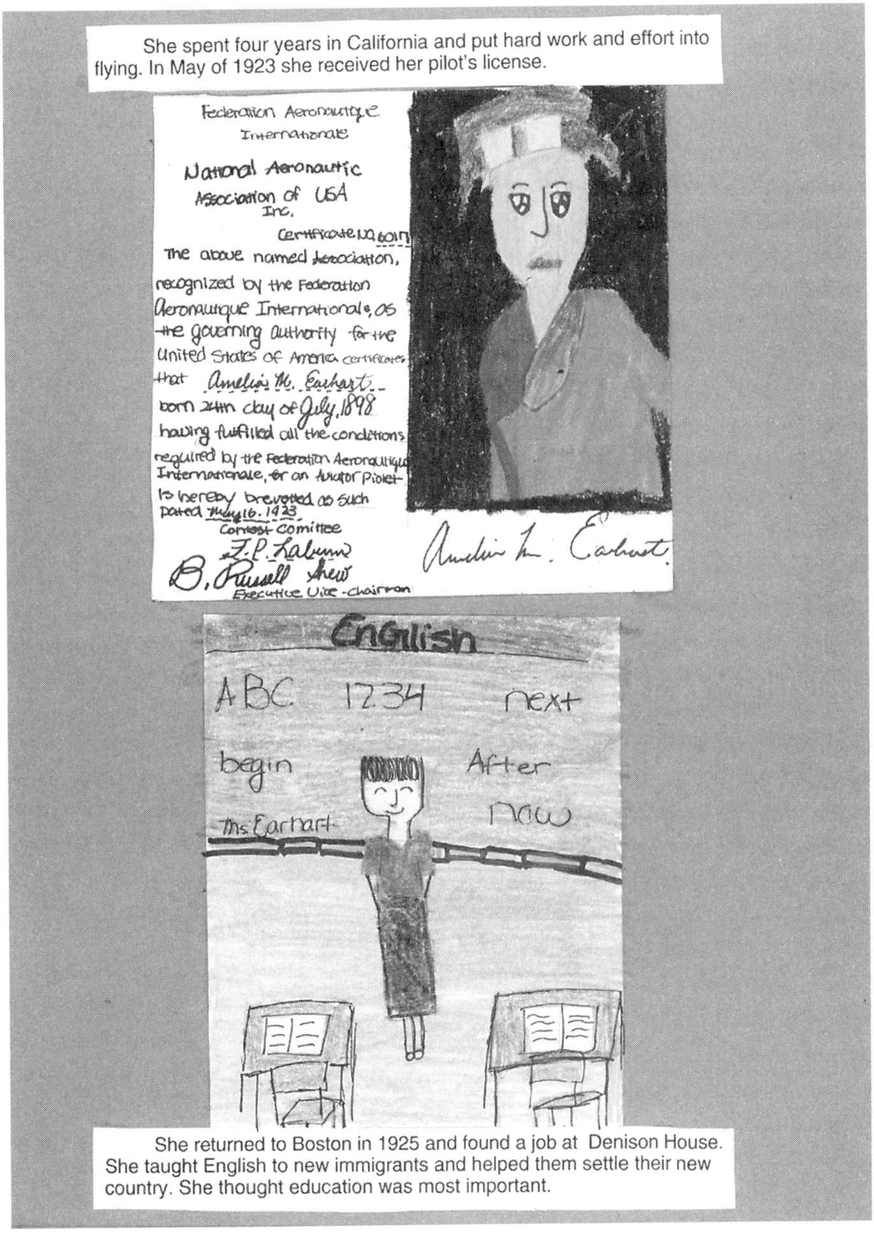

She spent four years in California and put hard work and effort into flying. In May of 1923 she received her pilot's license.

She returned to Boston in 1925 and found a job at Denison House. She taught English to new immigrants and helped them settle their new country. She thought education was most important.

FIGURE 5–1B Amelia Earhart Biography with Sidebar

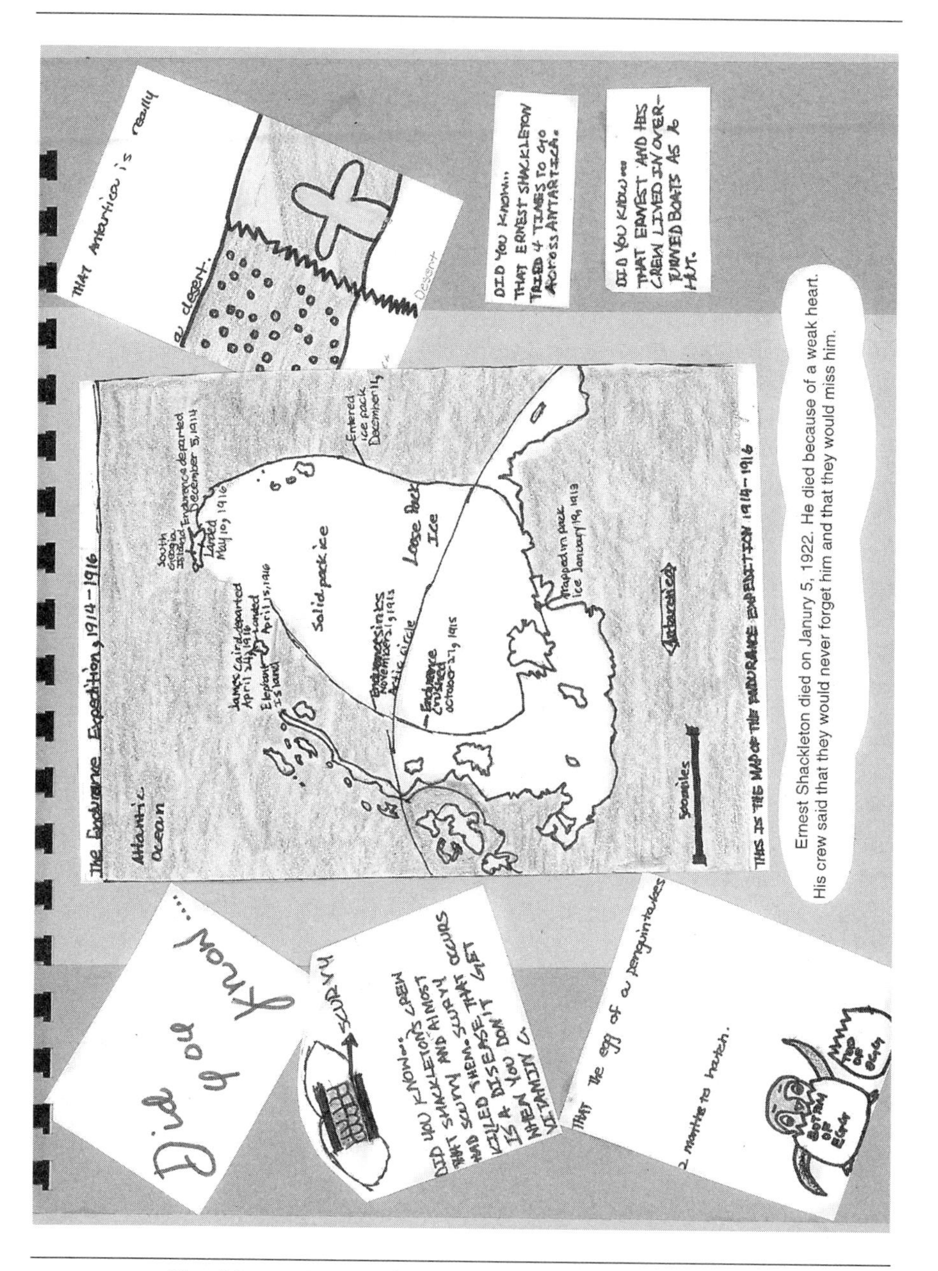

FIGURE 5–2 Shackleton Biography with Sidebars

FIGURE 5–3 Amelia Earhart Biography with Sidebar that Extends an Illustration

of the page in order to connect itself to the illustration. Here Neta Snook, a pilot who will become Amelia's teacher, is introduced next to a picture showing Amelia's growing fascination with airplanes.

The students found working with sidebars easy and appealing. Since most of their sidebars consisted of additional information, in the future I would make an effort to encourage students to also include definitions of important vocabulary words and quotations from the subject of the biography. Despite this, I am still pleased with the changing look of the biographies.

Captions

Captions provide young writers with another option for adding information and comment. By closely examining captions—the explanatory words writers add to identify and elaborate on illustrations—we can get a good idea of how authors are currently using them. What, exactly are they doing? How do captions join illustrations and written text?

One writer we can learn a great deal from, Jim Murphy, suggests that captions must be more than self-evident labels. In an interview, Murphy explained why interesting captions have long been important to him:

> When I was young, the first thing I looked at were the pictures and then I would read the captions. I clearly remember seeing a photograph of a cowboy on a horse in the desert. The caption said, "A cowboy riding a horse in the desert." I remember thinking, I can see that. What is the point of the caption? (Murphy in Kerper, 2000)

Like Murphy, our students may think they aren't going to learn anything new from captions. Why bother reading them if they offer nothing new or interesting? Why bother writing them if they will only annoy readers? The answer is, of course, that captions can offer more. Writers need to know what the options are, and then they need to practice integrating words and illustrations (Kerper, in press; Portalupi & Fletcher, 2001). This requires teaching.

In order to identify the qualities of interesting captions, I closely examined the captions in Jim Murphy's *Across America on an Emigrant Train* (1993) and *The Great Fire* (1995). I also looked at the captions in John Fleischman's *Phineas Gage* (2002) because I had been impressed while reading the book by how several captions suggested comparing one illustration with another. Fleischman had me paging back and forth as I read. Clearly, he was doing more than labeling.

Here's what I noticed. Murphy and Fleischman used captions to do at least six different things, using specific language to signal what they were doing. They used captions to:

- point out details we might not have noticed ("Notice that. . . .")
- give additional information beyond what is in either the text or the illustration
- give opinions
- speculate ("A likely explanation . . ."; "It's possible that . . .")
- refer to other illustrations in the book ("Compare this picture to . . .")
- pose a question ("Did . . . ?)

They also used relational terms to direct the reader's attention—words like *foreground, background, center, to the left, to the right, above,* and *below.* With these techniques and words, Murphy and Fleischman made their captions meaningful—something not to pass over.

Using these books, I shared several examples of captions with the fifth graders. Together, we discussed and listed the possible ways they, too, could use captions in their biographies. In this way, they were learning *how* to integrate visual material into their biographies. The content they chose to write about was still in their hands, but some proven options for shaping this content had been identified and made available. Other books besides the three that I used might turn up additional techniques. It's definitely worth extending the search.

Did students use these options to write meaningful captions? The encouraging news is that they did. While the students I worked with did not use all the techniques I shared with them, they used some. Several students took steps towards incorporating the language needed to direct a reader's attention to the details of an illustration. Others took the opportunity to share an opinion or speculate. Figure 5–4 shows examples of the captions they wrote to accompany their illustrations.

Timelines

Timelines have become more elaborate, providing authors with the opportunity to add illustrations and additional written material. Again, looking at the literature, I found four types to introduce:

1. *The Illustrated Timeline.* With this type of timeline, each date and event listed is accompanied by an illustration. This timeline reminds me of a slide presentation, with words and pictures

Using Relational Terms to Direct a Reader's Attention

- This is a picture of Antarctica. *Notice that* the South Pole lies in the middle of Antarctica [italics added].
- *Notice* behind Shackelton and his house there is a castle [italics added].
- Emily Dorman (*right*) was married with [*sic*] Shackelton (*left*) in 1904. [italics added].

Sharing an Opinion

- Amelia is the first woman to make a solo flight across the Atlantic. She did an excellent job for a pilot of that time.
- It was a horrible sight to the *Endurance* packed with ice and sinking.

Speculating

- Amelia landed right in a little village near Mexico City. She must have shocked them.
- In 1908, in Iowa, when Amelia was 11 years old, she went to Iowa State Fair. She saw her firts plane and wasn't impressed at all. It was a rusty metal and she probably even preferred pony rides. She must have hated the rusty plane.

FIGURE 5–4 Captions Written by Students

working together. A book like *The Secrets of Vesuvius* (Bisel, 1990) contains such a timeline entitled "The Buried Town Through the Ages." Together, words and illustrations show how Mt. Vesuvius has affected the town of Herculaneum between A.D. 79 and 1990.

2. *The Flow Diagram Timeline.* This type of timeline uses an actual path, what has been called an "arrow of time" (Moline, 1995, p. 80) to show time moving along. Although events are placed along the timeline, no attempt is made to segment it into equal intervals of time, say ten-year periods. In *Remember the Ladies: 100 Great American Women* (Harness, 2001), a timeline entitled "Down the Years with the Ladies" uses a winding blue river of time along which the contributions of various women are listed and illustrated. This timeline meanders across two full pages.

3. *The Graph-Like Timeline.* This timeline incorporates the features of a bar graph. In *Ghosts of the White House* (Harness, 1998), the life spans and terms of office for each president are shown, one underneath the other, like bars on a bar graph underneath a timeline shown at the top of the page. In this way, you can immediately see the years when each president served, who served two terms and who served even less than one, and how the life spans of the various presidents overlapped.
4. *Timeline Plus Quotations.* This timeline combines one or more relevant quotations, usually the words of the subject of the biography, with each date and event. At the end of *Malcolm X: A Fire Burning Brightly* (Myers, 2000), one of the dates and events listed in the timeline is "1947–1952. In prison, Malcolm becomes an avid reader and converts to Islam" (unpaged). One of the quotes that follows this is "My alma mater was books, a good library" (unpaged). Hearing Malcolm X speak for himself adds to our understanding of this man.

The fifth-grade students mostly opted to create an illustrated timeline when writing their biographies. Although there was some variation in the placement of the illustrations, dates, and events, the structure was largely the same (see Figures 5–5 and 5–6). One interesting twist on this was a timeline that coded the events as "very extremely important," "very important," or "important" (see Figure 5–7). At first this seemed very clever and amusingly childlike to me, but this morning as I was reading *The New York Times*, I came across a colorful, illustrated timeline entitled "A Tentative History of the Universe" (Overbye, 2002) and this timeline was coded for cosmological eras, major theories, and remaining questions. Because I saw how much information was packed into the newspaper timeline, I now see that what the student was doing—coding a timeline—can be further developed to include not only personal evaluations like "very extremely important" but also categories of information like "remaining questions." The literature (including newspapers) continues to present us with new options.

Authors' Notes

Authors' notes make us more aware of the person writing a biography. We gain insight into the actual person who became intrigued with the subject, did extensive research—perhaps traveling to various parts of the country or to other parts of the world—and who, in the end, thought

Time Line- Sir Ernest Shackleton

1874	Ernest Shackleton is born.
1901	Joins the National Antarctic Expedition led by Robert Falcon Scott.
1902	Shackleton, Scott, and Wilson get closer to the South Pole than anyone
1909	Shackleton and three other men get withen 97 miles from the South Pole.
1909	Shackleton is knighted Sir Ernest Shackleton.
1911	A Norwegian named Ronald Amundsen reaches the South Pole.
1914	Starts his third expedition on *Endurance*.
1915	*Endurance* becomes frozen in an ice pack and sinks.
1921	Shackleton sails on his fourth expedition on *Quest*.
1922	Shackleton dies on *Quest* which was off South Georgia.

FIGURE 5–5 Illustrated Timeline—Sir Ernest Shackleton

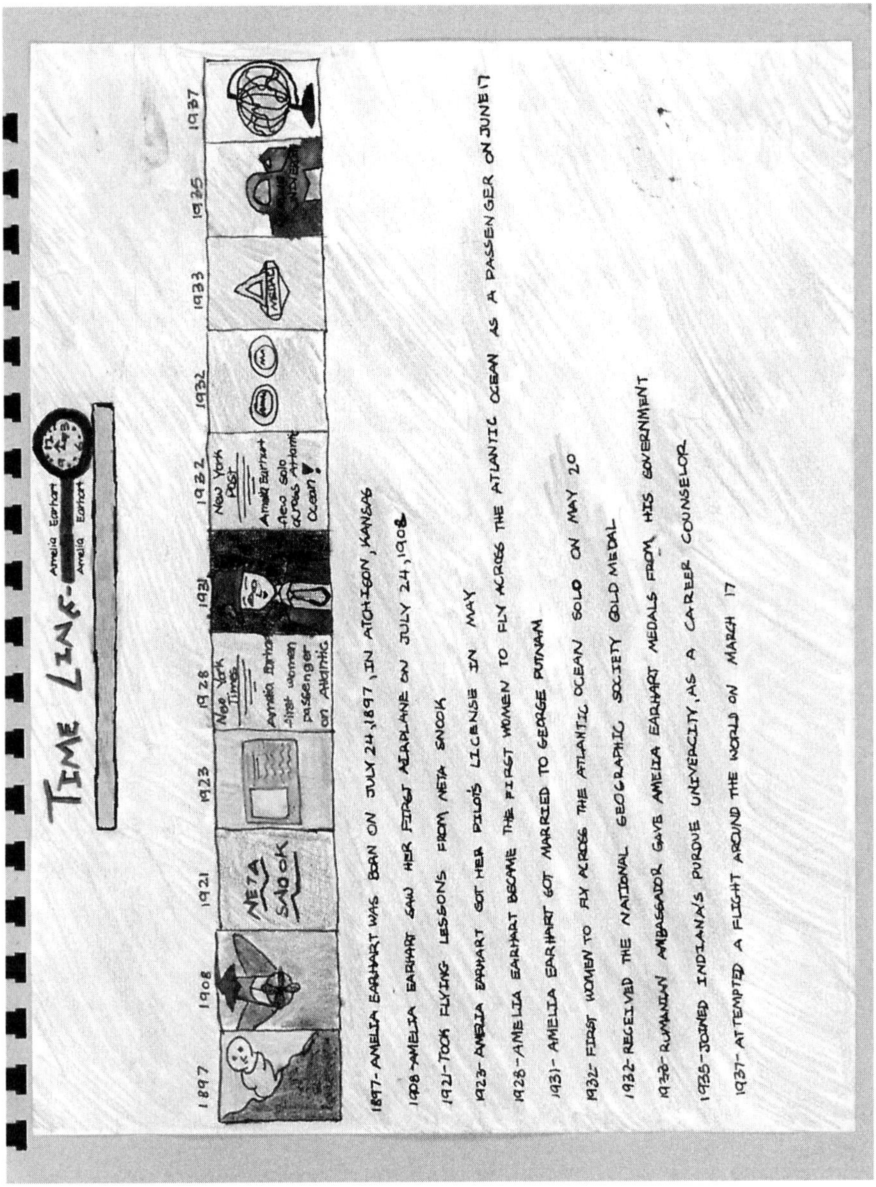

TIME LINE- Amelia Earhart

1897 1908 1921 1923 1928 1931 1932 1932 1933 1935 1937

NETA SNOOK

New York Times
Amelia Earhart first women passenger on Atlantic

New York Post
Amelia Earhart new solo across Atlantic Ocean!

MEDAL

1897- AMELIA EARHART WAS BORN ON JULY 24, 1897, IN ATCHISON, KANSAS
1908-AMELIA EARHART SAW HER FIRST AIRPLANE ON JULY 24, 1908
1921-TOOK FLYING LESSONS FROM NETA SNOOK
1923- AMELIA EARHART GOT HER PILOT'S LICENSE IN MAY
1928-AMELIA EARHART BECAME THE FIRST WOMEN TO FLY ACROSS THE ATLANTIC OCEAN AS A PASSENGER ON JUNE 17
1931- AMELIA EARHART GOT MARRIED TO GEORGE PUTNAM
1932- FIRST WOMEN TO FLY ACROSS THE ATLANTIC OCEAN SOLO ON MAY 20
1932-RECEIVED THE NATIONAL GEOGRAPHIC SOCIETY GOLD MEDAL
1933-RUMANIAN AMBASSADOR GAVE AMELIA EARHART MEDALS FROM HIS GOVERNMENT
1935-JOINED INDIANA'S PURDUE UNIVERCITY, AS A CAREER COUNSELOR
1937- ATTEMPTED A FLIGHT AROUND THE WORLD ON MARCH 17

FIGURE 5–6 Illustrated Timeline—Amelia Earhart

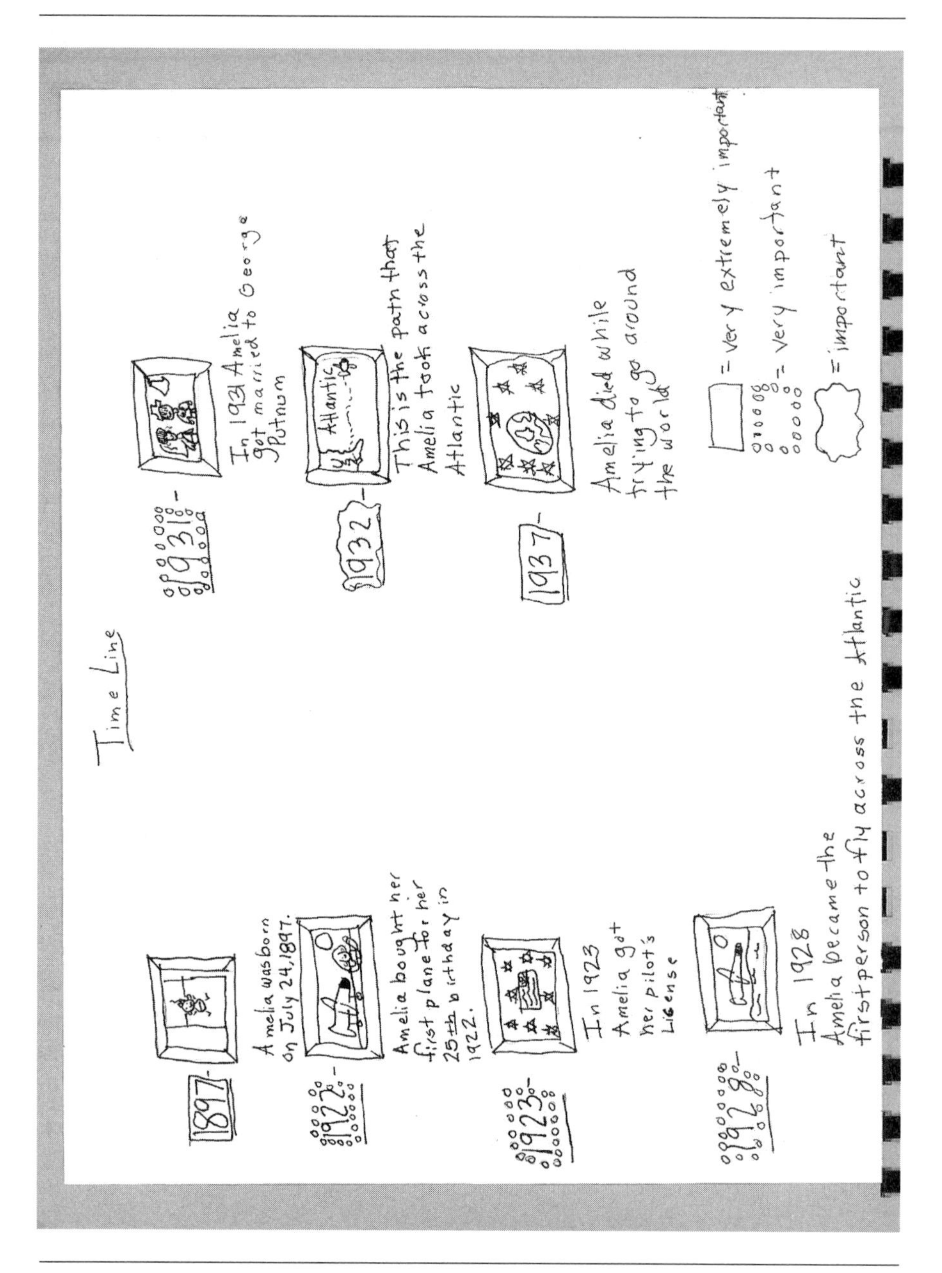

FIGURE 5–7 Coded Timeline

about what it all meant. Authors' notes reveal intentions, motivations, discoveries, frustrations—the human presence in the endeavor.

Authors' notes also provide information about the historical context. Authors writing for young readers know they are responsible for helping the reader connect with the past. An author's note acts as a bridge between the known and the unknown, bringing an unclear and unfamiliar setting into focus.

When looking at authors' notes with fifth graders, I wanted to give them a sense of these two aspects of the notes—first, providing a sense of the person behind the book and second, reaching out to readers and helping them connect with the historical context. These understandings would help students in their own reading and writing. As readers, a growing awareness of authors' notes would reinforce the idea that biography involves more than just gathering facts; readers should also expect to see creative thinking and thoughtful interpretation of the facts. As writers, students should think of the author's note as an opportunity to explain and document their own involvement in shaping the facts to create a biography.

Once again, literature provides the necessary models. Whether you are studying biography or reading multicultural literature, teachers are finding that authors' notes supply information about the "author's background and intentions in creating the book" and are "supplementary notes [that] set a person, place or event in a social, cultural, historical, and political context" (Perini, 2002, p. 429). When readers read these notes, their reading is enhanced.

In *Pick & Shovel Poet: The Journeys of Pascal D'Angelo* (2000) by Jim Murphy, a short introduction entitled "A Word About Pascal D'Angelo" is a fine example of an author sharing his personal involvement with his subject. Murphy tells readers that he was first drawn to Pascal D'Angelo because he was fascinated by his written language. Though Pascal was an Italian immigrant, his writing in English was surprisingly formal. Even so, it managed to have "a charming rhythmical quality" (p. xi). Murphy found this language intriguing. Another reason he wanted to learn more about Pascal D'Angelo was because his mother, also an Italian immigrant, had come to the United States at about the same time as Pascal. Murphy was interested in knowing what her immigrant experience was like. Since she had died, learning about Pascal D'Angelo might answer some of his pressing questions.

A second example that reveals the person behind the book is the afterword to *This Land Was Made for You and Me: The Life and Songs of Woody Guthrie* (2002) by Elizabeth Partridge. The author tells how, when she was in the sixth grade, her teacher told her to mouth the words to "This Land is Your Land" because her singing was off key. It was a painful and humiliating experience. It was not until many years later, while researching the book about Woody Guthrie, that she attended a concert and heard Woody's son Arlo urge everyone to sing because, as he explained, there are no wrong notes. And so she sang out loud. According to the author, "I finally understood what he [Woody] was saying all along: music is for singing and feeling and hoping and knowing, not for getting right" (p. 203). On a personal level, Elizabeth Partridge learned some truths from studying the life and work of Woody Guthrie. In fact, the personal connection is so strong that in this afterword the author includes a picture of herself as a child when she traveled with her family across the country, echoing, in a way, Woody Guthrie's travels.

An author's note that provides supplementary information is Milton Meltzer's preface to *Ten Queens: Portraits of Women of Power* (1998). Meltzer readies the reader by explaining the "divine right of kings" and by defining the group of ten queens as women who wielded power themselves *not* as women simply married to a king. By asking us to imagine how a strong and successful queen would be viewed in her time, Meltzer prepares us for the backlash from jealous men in the ten portraits to follow.

Similarly, in the authors' note to *Ida B. Wells: Mother of the Civil Rights Movement* (Fradin & Fradin, 2000) the authors explain why Ida B. Wells, an important civil rights leader, is virtually unknown to many people. The authors suggest that one reason is that she was so outspoken she even alienated some black leaders. They didn't celebrate her the way they celebrated Rosa Parks and Martin Luther King. The authors prepare readers for learning about Wells by briefly highlighting her accomplishments. She helped form the NAACP, worked for women's suffrage, ran her own newspaper, led a powerful anti-lynching campaign, and wrote articles and books demanding justice for African Americans. With this information, readers are ready to fill in the gaps in their knowledge about the civil rights movement. They are ready to read the book.

After the students I worked with examined authors' notes to see how they provided information about the person behind the book and provided supplementary information about the historical context, we discussed how they might approach writing their own authors' notes. We agreed on three questions they would use to guide their efforts.

Author's Note

Amelia Earhart was a famous pilot in the 1800's to the 1930's. She inspired many pilots to try their best. She was an extreme person; this means she would take many risks. Amelia Earhart once said, "Please know am quite aware of the hazards. I want to do it because I want to do it. Women must try things as men have tried. When they fail, their failure must be but a challenge to others." She made women's rights more available for others. Only a few women worked in those days. Now women take it for granted, but in those days women were thought crazy if they wanted certain jobs, such as flying.

In the book A Snapshot Biography of Amelia Earhart , it gives a general overview of Amelia Earhart's life with some side bars and pictures. The two sources I used were Sky Pioneer: A Photobiography of Amelia Earhart by Corinne Szabo and Amelia Earhart: Pioneer of the Sky by John Parlin.

I chose to write about Amelia Earhart because she was a great help to everybody. She was a fascinating woman because she was creative and did not have any boundaries put on her. Flying took a lot of courage and bravery. She was willing to risk her life to accomplish her missions.

FIGURE 5–8 Author's Note

1. Why is the person you are writing about interesting and important?
2. How did you find out about this person?
3. Why did you decide to write about this person?

You can see these questions reflected in the author's note shown in Figure 5-8 on page 87.

Putting It All Together

Putting all these pieces together to make one unified biography was an appealing project for intermediate grade children. I know this because I observed the children working busily over the course of several weeks for hours at a time. But one incident stands out in my mind. One girl's mother took her out of class to attend a graduation while we were working on these biographies. A few hours later, she brought her back, telling me that even though she had offered to take her daughter out to lunch and let her stay out of school for the remainder of the day, her daughter insisted on coming back to school.

One reason children found this project interesting was because they used multiple ways of constructing meaning. Sidebars, graphics, captions, illustrations, timelines, and authors' notes offered different opportunities for working with information. These "what else?" or "radical change" features required planning to see how they might work together. It required thinking about how to best present information—as part of the main text, a sidebar, an illustration, a caption, an author's note, or a timeline. It even involved incorporating information—particularly in sidebars—that might otherwise have been left out, but now had a place. All of this planning and piecing together allowed for originality.

A look at one completed biography (see Figure 5–9) shows how all the pieces fit together. As you read this biography of Amelia Earhart, think about the different ways the information is presented. Also think about how you went about putting the different pieces of information together. Did you proceed in a linear way? Did you skip around, moving back and forth? Did you feel more active as a reader? Did you like having these choices? These questions arise because of the presence of "what else?" features.

A Look Ahead

The way biography is written is evolving. Newer features, like the ones discussed in this chapter, are enhancing and invigorating older ways of

FIGURE 5–9 Complete Biography—The Amazing Life of Amelia Earhart

FIGURE 5–9 *Continued*

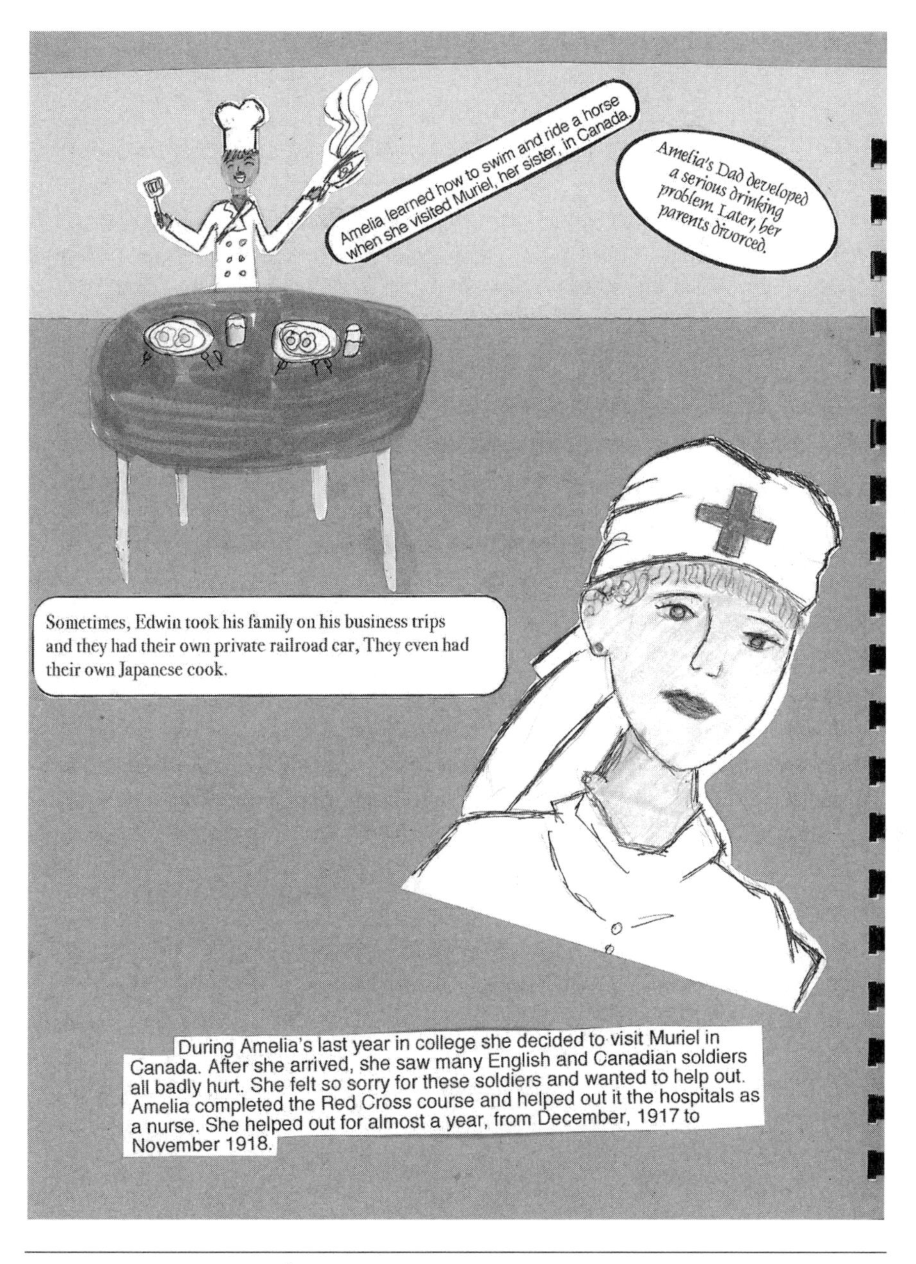

FIGURE 5–9 *Continued*

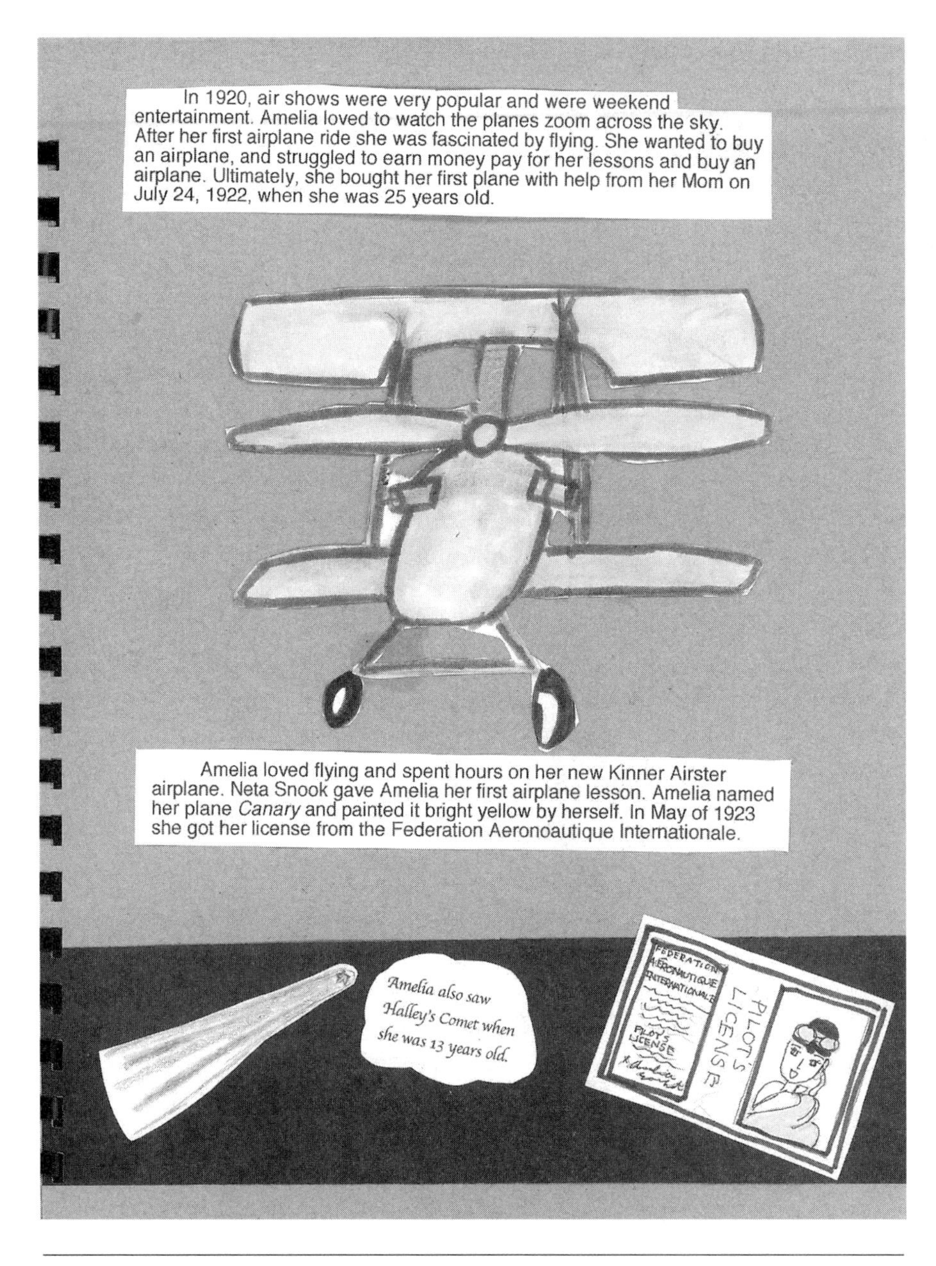

FIGURE 5–9 *Continued*

FIGURE 5–9 *Continued*

FIGURE 5–9 *Continued*

The flight on the *Friendship*, as a passenger, influenced Amelia a lot to fly solo across the Atlantic. On May 20, 1932 she was ready for the challenge. At dusk, from Harbor Grace, Newfoundland, she took off and landed 13 hours and 30 minutes later in Londonderry, Ireland. She became the first woman to fly successfully solo across the Atlantic Ocean.

The Solo Flight across the Atlantic

FIGURE 5–9 *Continued*

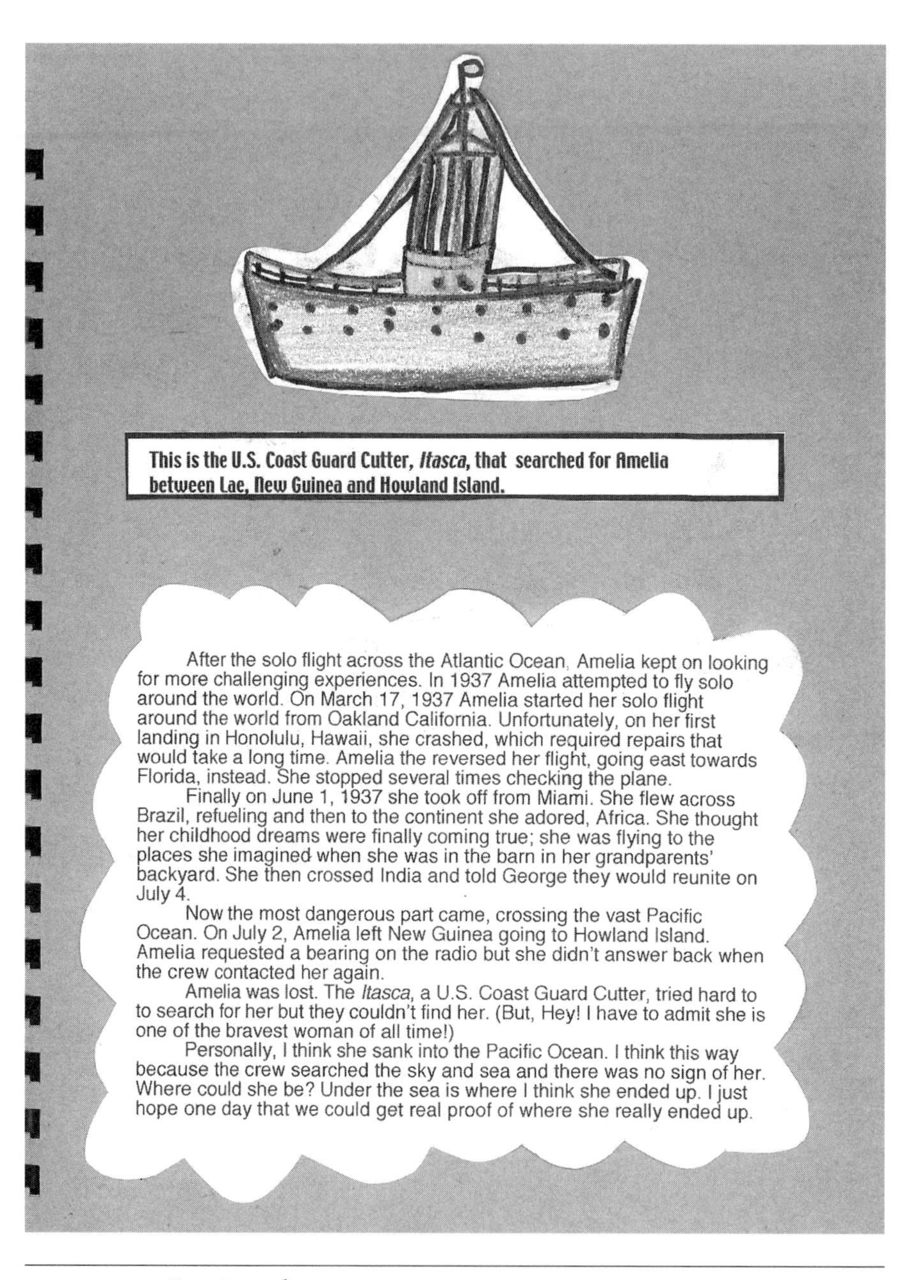

FIGURE 5–9 *Continued*

FIGURE 5–9 *Continued*

FIGURE 5–9 *Continued*

Author's Note

Amelia Earhart was a brave and adventurous person. She was always determined to reach her goal even if it meant death. She was independent, active and kind to others.

I used three books for my research. I used Sky Pioneer by Corine Szabo for most of my information, Lost Star by Partricia Launber and Amelia Earhart by John Parlin for additional information.

My teacher chose the assignment for me, though I really enjoyed learning about Amelia Earhart's life and was fascinated by the things she did. I hope when you read my book you will also be fascinated by the extraordinary life of Amelia Earhart!

FIGURE 5–9 *Continued*

AMELIA
EARHART

Jing Jing Sun

US $4.95
CAN$5.95

FIGURE 5–9 *Continued*

writing biography. It is likely that we will be seeing even more changes in the future. In a recent interview, author and editor James Cross Giblin (Harris & McCarthey, 2002) suggested that one as yet untried way of approaching biography is to present multiple perspectives on a subject. He suggested that a book about Thomas Jefferson could have segments written from the point of view of a steadfast admirer, a slave, and a writer-editor seeking a balanced overview of Jefferson's life. He also suggested that biographies could incorporate different kinds of nonprint material. It's not hard to imagine a biography accompanied by a CD or video.

Even within current biographies, authors are raising new questions and offering new ways of presenting life stories. The next chapter examines some of these questions.

Additional Sources with Sidebars, Captions, Timelines, and Authors' Notes

More and more biographies and histories are incorporating "what else?" features. Below is a sampling of titles which, in addition to the titles already mentioned in the chapter, would make excellent models to study. Many of these books have more than one "what else?" feature that could prompt a discussion of how these features work together.

Sidebars

Goodman, J. E. (2001). *Despite All Obstacles: La Salle and the Conquest of the Mississippi*. New York: Mikaya. [48 pp.]
While chronicling La Salle's travels down the Mississippi, the author also provides sidebars with excerpts from the writings of La Salle and others who knew him. This book clearly shows how to use sidebars to add relevant primary sources such as letters, speeches, and eyewitness accounts.

Greenberg, J., and S. Jordan. (2000). *Frank O. Gehry: Outside In*. New York: DK. [48 pp.]
In this book focused on the work of the architect Frank O. Gehry, who designed the Guggenheim Museum in Bilbao, Spain, the innovative use of graphics and sidebars matches Gehry's own innovative style. One sidebar, for example, is totally visual, providing different views of one of his constructions. Readers should take some time to also study the innovative use of bold, colorful print in this book.

Meltzer, Milton. (2002) *Ten Kings and the Worlds They Ruled.* Illustrated by B. Andersen. New York: Scholastic/Orchard. [144 pp.]
This companion book to *Ten Queens* mentioned in this chapter focuses on how kings have used their powers. Sidebars with additional information are incorporated into the ten portraits.

Captions

These titles from the highly visual National Geographic Photobiography series have extensive captions accompanying large reproductions of maps and photographs. In addition, each book integrates quotations from the subject, setting them off from the main text by printing them in a different color and font. Authors of these books also use many relational terms (e.g., left, right, top, bottom) when discussing the illustrations.

Bausum, A. (2000). *Dragon Bones and Dinosaur Eggs: A Photobiography of Roy Chapman Andrews.* Washington, DC: National Geographic. [64 pp.]
Coburn, B. (2000). *Triumph on Everest: A Photobiography of Sir Edmund Hillary.* Washington, DC: National Geographic. [64 pp.]
Matthews, T. L. (1999). *Always Inventing: A Photobiography of Alexander Graham Bell.* Washington, DC: National Geographic. [64 pp.]
Matthews, T. L. (1998). *Light Shining Through the Mist: A Photobiography of Dian Fossey.* Washington, DC: National Geographic. [64 pp.]
Salkeld, A. (2000). *Mystery on Everest: A Photobiography of George Mallory.* Washington, DC: National Geographic. [64 pp.]

Timelines

Harness, C. (1996). *They're Off! The Story of the Pony Express.* New York: Simon & Schuster. [32 pp.]
In an unusual "take" on time, the author-illustrator presents an illustrated list of events that took place in different parts of the world during the time the Pony Express was in operation. Entitled "Around the World in the Days of the Pony Express," the illustrations and words form a frame around the last page of the book. In the center of the page is a bibliography.

Hehner, B. (1999). *First on the Moon.* Illustrated by G. Ruhl. New York: Hyperion. [48 pp.]
A double-page spread details "Milestones in Space" using an illustrated timeline that proceeds year by year from 1957 through 1998. The timeline is color-coded to show the different space flights—Mercury, Gemini, Apollo, and Space Shuttle.

Kurlansky, M. (2001). *The Cod's Tale*. Illustrated by S.D. Schindler. New York: Putnam. [46 pp.]
Since this book is based on the author's adult book, *Cod: A Biography of the Fish That Changed the World*, perhaps we can consider this book, too, to be a biography. Flow diagram timelines appear on the tops or bottoms of many of the pages. Also, check out the sidebars, many of which deal with unusual ways of preparing cod, including a recipe for codfish "tongues" and cod-head chowder.

Authors' Notes

Kerley, B. (2001). *The Dinosaurs of Waterhouse Hawkins*. Illustrated by B. Selznick. New York: Scholastic. [48 pp.]
An author's note that ends this Caldecott award-winning book tells how the author first became interested in Waterhouse Hawkins and provides additional information about his life and times. An artist's note follows in which artist Brian Selznick explains the research he did in the process of illustrating this book.

Pinkney, A. D. (2000). *Let It Shine: Stories of Black Women Freedom Fighters*. Illustrated by S. Alcorn. San Diego: Harcourt. [107 pp.]
In a note entitled "This Little Light of Mine," the author credits her family's continuing involvement with the civil rights movement as contributing to her commitment to civil rights. Pinkney explains that her motivation for writing this book stems from this commitment. She also discusses the difficult process of selecting just ten women to write about.

Tallchief, M., and R. Wells. (1999). *Tallchief: America's Prima Ballerina*. Illustrated by G. Kelley. New York: Viking. [28 pp.]
In an author's note that begins the book, Rosemary Wells introduces readers to the ballerina Maria Tallchief and then tells why she chose to write about her. Wells first learned about the dancer from her mother, who at one time belonged to the same ballet company as Tallchief. The author's personal connection to her subject stems from the stories her mother told her about Tallchief, who she considered to be America's greatest ballet dancer.

Zaunders, B. (1998). *Crocodiles, Camels, and Dugout Canoes: Eight Adventurous Episodes*. Illustrated by Roxie Munro. New York: Dutton. [48 pp.]
In a preface that opens the book, the authors explain how the idea for the book took shape, and how the eight adventurers were selected from

a much larger list of possible subjects. A major consideration for both the author and illustrator was finding adventurers who also wrote extensively about their exploits and were amateur adventurers, not professionals. There's a great deal of information about the writing process in this brief two-page note.

6
Simple Questions Without Simple Answers

In previous chapters I have suggested taking a questioning stance when reading biography. I considered some seemingly simple questions:

- **What if?** I reported how students who read the biography of Ruby Bridges were able to identify turning points in her story—times when important decisions had been made. They asked, "What if a different decision had been made by Ruby, her family, school personnel, or government officials in Louisiana?" Would the course of school integration have turned out differently?
- **What's the difference?** I showed how students who read three biographies of the same subject learned about historical interpretation. They asked, "What's the difference between *A Picture Book of Benjamin Franklin* (Adler, 1990), *What's the Big Idea, Ben Franklin?* (Fritz, 1976), and *The Amazing Life of Ben Franklin*?" (Giblin, 2000). Using these books they noticed how different authors and illustrators selected, interpreted, and presented information about Franklin.
- **What do I think?** I explained how students responded to the challenge of a visible author. Diane Stanley challenged readers to consider the meaning of Joan of Arc's claim that she saw visions and heard voices. Students accepted this challenge and vigorously defended the positions they took. They asked themselves, "What do I think about Joan's claim that she saw visions and heard voices?"
- **What else?** I showed how students who studied the life of either Amelia Earhart or Sir Ernest Shackleton were able to supplement the main narrative with additional information. They asked, "Besides the information in the main narrative, what else can I include about the person or the times in which he or she lived?"

They put additional information in sidebars, timelines, captions, and authors' notes.

With these simple questions, I launched in-depth inquiries that grabbed the attention of middle-grade students and opened up the study of biography to critical examination. Why? Because these simple questions don't have simple answers. They are questions we can't immediately solve. We need to walk around with them for a while, turning over different possible answers in our minds.

Why are students willing to do this? Because these questions, like ordinary puzzles, are challenging. It's the same reason that many people read mysteries, do crossword puzzles, watch all sorts of quiz shows trying to outguess the contestants, and even look for Waldo in the crowded pictures of *Where's Waldo?* (1997). It's the puzzling question or challenge that's motivating, whether we're in kindergarten, graduate school, or beyond.

This is true not only for biography and history, but for other subjects as well. Several years ago, my colleague Frances Curcio and I asked children who had read a poem by Shel Silverstein about a library book that was forty-two years overdue, how they could figure out the fine (Curcio, Zarnowski, & Vigliarolo, 1995). They were happily occupied for days with this problem, using calculators and making charts. They used a number of different problem-solving strategies.

Creating a puzzling situation is especially useful when teaching history. It's what good history teachers report doing when they design challenging activities. To learn about the "real" Pilgrim experience, Monica Edinger asked her fourth-grade students to read *Mourt's Relation*, a document written by the Pilgrims and published in 1622. She describes reading primary source documents with children as "very challenging," but also "very stimulating and exciting" (2000, p. 6). During a unit on the American Revolution, James Percoco asked high school students, "In your opinion, is the American Revolution over?" (2001, p. 25). In order to give them a sense of the complexity of the topic, Percoco introduced students to relevant art, literature, film and video, and primary source documents. Bruce VanSledright challenged fifth graders to become history detectives and try to figure out what happened in Jamestown during the Starving Time. He reported that "students appeared intrigued by the prospect of solving the mystery" (2002, p. 41). The common ingredient in all these examples is that teachers raised simple questions without simple answers.

What was the Pilgrim experience like? Is the American Revolution over? What happened during the Starving Time? The questions are straightforward; the answers are not.

Good questions are not in short supply. Because I am always on the alert for intriguing questions raised by biographers, I am often able to find them. The next section deals with some of my finds.

Biographers As Questioners: Some Intriguing Models

The questions biographers raise for themselves provide a focus for their research and writing. Biographers seem to be asking themselves, "What issues in a life story do I find most interesting? What issues seem relevant in today's world?" In addition, when they are writing for children, biographers are likely to ask themselves, "What do children want to know? What background information do they need to know?" Their completed biographies reflect the answers they discover. You can see this in the work of Kathleen Krull, Russell Freedman, Kathryn Lasky, and Diane Stanley. The questions they raise are interesting to think about.

Kathleen Krull: Asking Nosy Questions

The lively *Lives of . . .* series written by Kathleen Krull and illustrated by Kathryn Hewitt takes a decidedly "gossipy" stance. Author Kathleen Krull asks questions that are "respectful but definitely nosy" (1998, p. 9) in order to find the more human side of famous people. In the introduction to *Lives of Extraordinary Women* (2000), she asks, "Are they so different from us? What were they like as human beings? What might their neighbors have noticed?" (p. 9). In *Lives of the Presidents* (1998), she points out that unlike other books, hers will deal with "hairstyles, attitudes, diets, bad habits, ailments, fears, money, sleep patterns, and underwear" (p. 9). In *Lives of Athletes* (1997), she asks, "What were they like as people? Were their actions in private always so sportsmanlike? And were they as popular with their neighbors as with their fans?" (p. 9). In an article about this series in *Book Links*, Krull summed up these books by saying, "The 'Lives of . . .' books, while scrupulously researched, are a sort of *People Magazine* of nonfiction . . ." (Krull, 1999, p. 21). They use gossip as a means of grabbing readers' attention and introducing them to some of the world's greatest achievers.

Look at the following titles and subtitles of the books in this series.

- *Lives of Extraordinary Women: Rulers, Rebels (and What the Neighbors Thought)*
- *Lives of the Presidents: Fame, Shame (and What the Neighbors Thought)*
- *Lives of the Athletes: Thrills, Spills (and What the Neighbors Thought)*
- *Lives of Artists: Masterpieces, Messes (and What the Neighbors Thought)*
- *Lives of the Writers: Comedies, Tragedies (and What the Neighbors Thought)*
- *Lives of Musicians: Good Times, Bad Times (and What the Neighbors Thought)*

As you can see, "what the neighbors thought," gets the same billing as being a powerful ruler, performing thrilling athletic feats, or creating great art. So do the goofs—the shameful behavior, messes, bad times, and mistakes. This series doesn't sweep the unusual or even unflattering bits of information under the carpet. It revels in them.

The twenty or so portraits in each volume of the *Lives of . . .* series (more for the presidents) have an unusual mix of information. Nosy questions yield nosy answers. As you might expect, the information is personal and the style is friendly and good-humored. Reading the portraits in these books, I get the feeling that the author is whispering in my ear. She seems to be saying, "You'll never guess what!" or "Listen to this!" That's because she uses parentheses to insert juicy details. When introducing Catherine the Great, empress of Russia, she says, "She wasn't even Russian (though it was rumored that she'd asked her doctor to drain her blood and replace it with that of a Russian)" (Krull, 2000, p. 37). To introduce George Washington she tells us, "At six feet two inches, George Washington had big muscles, big moves (always elegant and powerful), and big feet (size thirteen)" (Krull, 1998, p. 11).

This powerful mix of "fame, shame, and what the neighbors thought" provides a balanced, more human portrait. Using any of the volumes in the *Lives of . . .* series, students can sort the information using the same categories that Krull does. For example, after reading about George Washington in *Lives of the Presidents: Fame, Shame (and What the Neighbors Thought)*, students can construct a chart using Krull's categories. The following is an example of the information Krull provides about Washington.

GEORGE WASHINGTON

Fame	Shame	What the Neighbors Thought
first president	poor speaker	brave
first millionaire	had a temper	boring
had stamina	wasn't fatherly	modest, shy
	wasn't dashing	excellent host
	wrote mushy love poetry	

There are lots of other personal details you can find in this portrait—the names of Washington's dogs, what he liked to eat for breakfast, and his attitude towards bathing, and more.

One concrete way to show that the questions we ask affect the answers we find is to compare Krull's "nosy" portrait of Washington in *Lives of the Presidents* with James Cross Giblin's *George Washington: A Picture Book Biography* (1992), which presents far less personal information. In Giblin's book the focus is on Washington as a military and political leader and as a devoted family man. Giblin's book is a fine biography for young readers, but there aren't too many "nosy" details in it. There are a few remarks about Washington's false teeth, but nothing like the amount of personal information in *Lives of the Presidents*.

Ask your students what they think of the nosy approach to biography. Are the details appealing? Is this a good way to tell a life story?

Russell Freedman: Returning to the Same Questions

In an author's note at the end of *Babe Didrikson Zaharias: The Making of a Champion* (1999), Russell Freedman puts a whole new slant on questioning: What happens when a biographer reexamines the life and times of a person he has written about before? Will new ideas emerge? Will the "facts" change? As Freedman tells us in his author's note, the answer to both of these questions is "yes."

Freedman first wrote about the famous athlete Babe Didrikson in his book *Teenagers Who Made History* in 1961. Almost forty years later, he wrote about her again. One change Freedman made to his material was factual. Although he had assumed that Babe had told the truth about her age, it was later determined that she often subtracted one or more years from her birthdate. At the time of the Olympics of 1932, Babe wasn't a teenager at all; she was twenty-one.

Compare the following excerpts from the two books to see how Freedman benefited from more recent scholarship in order to give Babe's correct age. In *Teenagers Who Made History,* he wrote:

> At the end of 1932, Babe was voted the Woman Athlete of the Year in the annual Associated Press poll. This surprised no one. As far as most people were concerned, the *18-year-old* Texas girl was the Woman Athlete of any year. [emphasis added] (pp. 166–67)

In *Babe Didrikson Zaharias*, he corrected Babe's age:

> *Although Babe turned twenty-one a few days before the games opened,* she was widely believed to be nineteen. On her application form for the Olympics she had fudged a bit, writing in her penciled girlish scrawl that she was born in 1913, rather than 1911. And when reporters hailed her as a teenage athletic marvel, she did not bother to correct them. [emphasis added] (p. 59)

Freedman even adds that because Babe had changed her age so many times over the years, at the time of her death reporters weren't sure how old she was. It's interesting to see how Freedman sets the factual record straight.

It's even more interesting to see that, over time, Freedman developed a different understanding of Babe's life. The theme of *Teenagers Who Made History* is Babe's competitiveness and how it led to her amazing achievements. Because she always wanted to be the best and to win every contest, she worked hard to hone her athletic skills. The newer book, while acknowledging this, has a much different theme. In *Babe Didrikson Zaharias* we learn that Babe's behavior, while seemingly radical and even outlandish for her time, would be considered quite normal by today's standards. Again, look at excerpts from the two books. The first, from *Teenagers,* highlights her competitive spirit:

> Though everyone in the family was athletically inclined, there was one thing about Babe that set her apart from her brothers and sister. *She was the most fiercely competitive of them all.* . . . "All my life," she once remarked, "I've had the urge to do things better than anyone else." [emphasis added] (p. 146)

This theme recurs when Babe first meets the team members of the Golden Cyclones, a women's basketball team she will be playing on. When a team member tells Babe she is the star forward and asks what position Babe wants to play, she replies: "Well, that's what I want to be" (p. 154).

In contrast, the theme of *Babe Didrikson Zaharias* is that Babe's behavior, while considered brash, loud, and just plain "over the top" during her lifetime, would seem normal by today's standards. Freedman makes the case that she was rising above restrictive ideas about how women should behave. In 1999, he writes:

> Babe had been snubbed not only because of her working-class background, but also because *she seemed to defy conventional notions of proper feminine behavior.* In an era when many people believed that women should be soft, submissive, and dependent, Babe Didrikson seemed all wrong. She was tough, resourceful, and independent. [emphasis added] (p. 96)

Freedman contrasts the behavior expected of a young women in the 1930s—"modest and demure" (p. 44)—with Babe's outspoken demeanor. He concludes, "Today, I don't think her behavior would seem so outrageous" (p. 56).

This is extraordinary material to share with students. I do not know of any other author of children's or young adult history or biography who has been so forthright about reinterpreting material. Placing the two books side by side allows us to ask, "What's changed in the way Russell Freedman thinks about Babe Didrikson? What causes a biographer like Freedman to change his mind, or to understand a life story in a different way? Why would a biographer revise his thinking?" Together, you and your students can collect quotes, like the ones I selected, to show these changes and to examine them more closely. This example of reinterpreting the past should not be missed. Even though *Teenagers Who Made History* is more than forty years old, I had no trouble finding it in my college library. It should be possible to get through interlibrary loan if your library doesn't have it.

If you want to continue with this topic, another book that deals with reinterpretation is Steven Jaffe's *Who Were the Founding Fathers? Two Hundred Years of Reinventing American History* (1996). In this book, Jaffe shows how over the course of time, Americans have seen our Founding Fathers in different ways. This is not the story of how one biographer changed his ideas, but of how different authors have seen the same people. According to Jaffe,

> People managed to find ideas and qualities in the lives of George Washington, Benjamin Franklin, and other revolutionary heroes that seemed to mirror their own concerns and hopes—even if the Founders themselves might not always have understood or accepted how later Americans saw them. (p. 6)

Like Russell Freedman, Steven Jaffe suggests that our present concerns influence how we think about the past. Do you and your students agree?

Kathryn Lasky: Asking Lingering Questions

A biography can begin with a question that lingers in the author's mind.

When Kathryn Lasky was a young girl growing up in Indianapolis, she ran a lemonade stand during the summer. One day when she came indoors with a jar of change, her mother commented that she might grow up to be the next Madam Walker. What is the connection between the young Kathryn Lasky and the black millionaire businesswoman?

In an author's note that begins *Vision of Beauty: The Story of Sarah Breedlove Walker* (2000), Lasky tells readers about the lemonade stand and her mother's comment. She also explains that as a child she had been fascinated by the successful Madam Walker. This fascination eventually grew into a picture book biography.

Lasky finds a lot to celebrate in the life of Madam Walker. Born the poor daughter of sharecroppers, Sarah Breedlove Walker became a millionaire by selling the hair care products she developed especially for black women. Madam Walker was interested in more than making money. She mixed business success with civic responsibility. She gave back to her community, helping many black women who worked for her to become economically independent. In addition, she gave to charities and encouraged her employees to do so too. Madam Walker was a strong, outspoken, civic-minded woman. No wonder Kathryn Lasky was able to build on her mother's chance comment and her early interest in Madam Walker's career. We can all learn about caring for oneself and others from Madam Walker's extraordinary career. The fact that Madam Walker also grew up in Kathryn Lasky's home town of Indianapolis further cemented the bond.

Like *Vision of Beauty,* Kathryn Lasky's picture book biography of the Greek mathematician Eratosthenes, *The Librarian Who Measured the Earth* (1994) also began with a lingering question. In an author's note to this book, Lasky tell readers that she first became interested in Eratosthenes while looking over her husband's research notes for a television program he was working on. In these notes she learned that Eratosthenes had figured out a way to measure the earth's circumference without the help of sophisticated instruments. How did he do this? She became curious, and that curiosity led to researching and writing a biography.

We can learn to tap the power of lingering questions the way Kathryn Lasky does. A couple of children's books can also assist us in introducing our students to the power of lingering questions. Jean Fritz's *George Washington's Breakfast* (Putnam, 1969) tells how a young boy named George Washington Allen just had to find out what George Washington ate for breakfast. After everyone else gives up, he continues to investigate

. . . and he ultimately finds the answer. Not only is his curiosity satisfied, but he gets a special breakfast. Along the way, author Jean Fritz tells readers about the process of research and celebrates the thrill of a successful find. Louise Bordon's *A. Lincoln and Me* (1999) is also about the connection a young boy feels for a president. In this book, a young boy who shares the same birthday as Lincoln is encouraged by his teacher to think about how much he is like the president. Like Lincoln, the boy is skinny and often clumsy. Yet, also like Lincoln, he is a reader, a leader, and a teller of funny jokes. Learning about Lincoln helps the boy learn to appreciate his own good qualities and accept his shortcomings. The boy's motivation to learn more about Lincoln is strong. At one point in the book, he remarks that there is a whole shelf of library books about Lincoln in his school library. The accompanying illustration shows him sitting next to a pile of books about Lincoln and he appears to be reading Russell Freedman's *Lincoln: A Photobiography.* Although the author never says it directly, the unstated message is that we can use the example of other people's lives to guide our own.

In the classroom, we can ask our students to follow up on their lingering questions. Is there someone fascinating whom they want to learn more about, like Kathryn Lasky did? Like the fictional George Washington Allen, do any students share a name with someone famous? Do they want to know more about that person? Like the boy in *A. Lincoln and Me,* do students share a birthday with someone famous in history?

Diane Stanley: Asking Unanswerable Questions

Again and again, as she writes a life story Diane Stanley highlights the gaps in available information, helping readers understand the limits of biography. It seems reasonable that we cannot know everything about a person's life down to the small details; yet, as Stanley shows readers, sometimes we do not have even the basic information. When writing about William Shakespeare she and co-author Peter Vennema might ask, "When was he born? What was he like as a boy? What did he do to earn money before he began writing plays?" Or when writing about Cleopatra they may wonder, "What did her friends and supporters have to say about her? What exactly did she look like? How did she die?" These are important questions, but there aren't any available answers.

Biographers and historians must rely on hedging—suggesting that *perhaps* this is what happened, *probably* it happened this way, or *it might have been* like this. Using terms like these—called hedges—they can make informed guesses. Hedging is a common practice when writing about the past because "historians are generally forced to deal with probabilities, not certainties . . ." (Davidson & Lytle, 1992, p. xxx). In the process they "leave an imprint" (p. xxxi) of their thoughts on the facts.

This practice of hedging, when authors show that they are not quite certain, is something that we need to pass along to students, and it needs to be done through the use of trade books, because trade book writers are more likely than textbook writers to use hedges. In a study comparing social studies textbooks with trade books written for adults, a researcher found that trade book writers "use more hedges perhaps because they keep in mind that history is memory of the past rather a record of the past and that many historians often disagree about issues . . ." (Crismore, 1984, p. 293). In effect, they present history in a truer, more discipline-specific way. This researcher even suggested that when authors leave out statements of what is probable, possible, or likely they make critical reading more difficult. How are young readers to separate what is fairly certain from what is not certain at all without help from the author? In fact, in a later study this researcher and her colleague (Crismore & Vande Kopple, 1988) found that students learned more from material that contained hedges. Instead of seeing words like *perhaps* and *probably* as "deadwood" or "clutter words" (p. 199), they suggest, we need to see them as promoting comprehension and historical understanding.

Many of Diane Stanley's books contain hedges that we can point out to students. In *Leonardo da Vinci* (1996), for example, readers learn that *probably* after his birth Leonardo lived with his mother, not his father. Stanley also explains that *probably* Leonardo learned about the beauties of nature from his uncle, and *probably* the village priest gave him some limited schooling. Commenting on his work habits, she notes that *no one knows why* he had a habit of starting projects and not finishing them. Even where Leonardo's remains are located, she tells us, is uncertain. A grave marked with his name *might be* his, but *probably* isn't.

We can ask students to look for hedging when reading biographies like *Leonardo, Bard of Avon,* or *Cleopatra.* Students can look for words and phrases that show uncertainty—like *it may have been, no one knows, it is likely, it seems that,* and *it is possible.* Students can use a web like the one shown in Figure 6–1 to collect examples of hedges in *Bard of Avon* and then to list information that is tentative and information that is certain. Studying examples of hedging shows students how an author tries to bridge the gaps between the known and the unknown by dealing with

BARD OF AVON by Diane Stanley and Peter Vennema

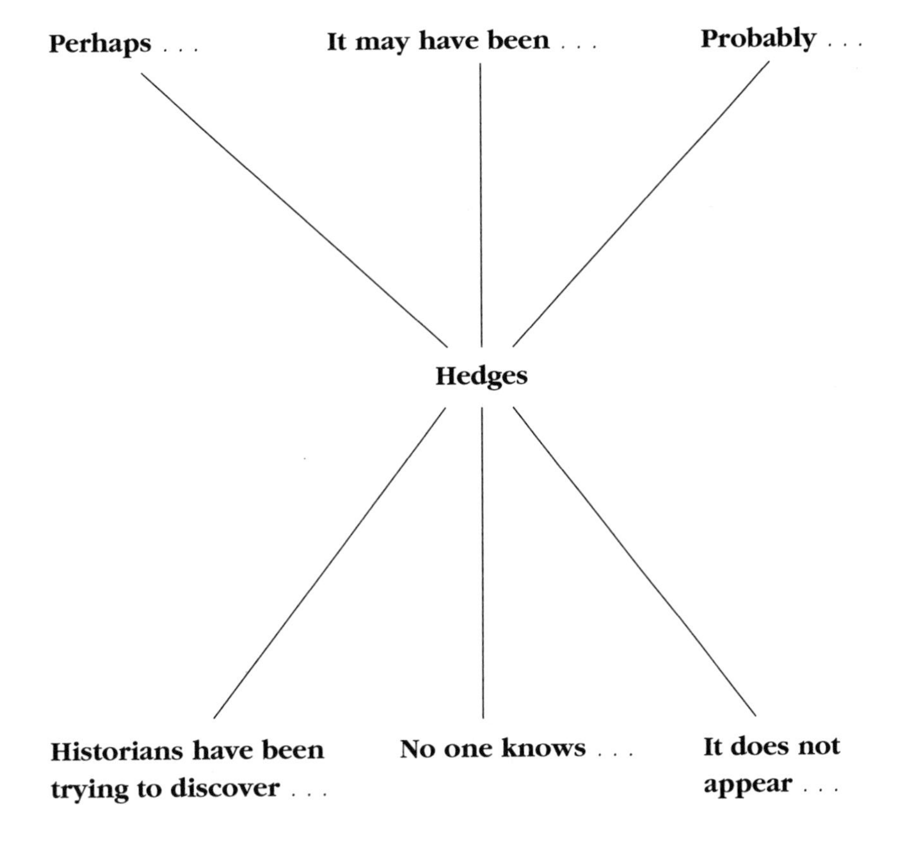

What We Don't Know or Aren't Sure of	*What We Do Know*

FIGURE 6–1 Finding Hedges

possibilities. What do you and your students think about hedging? Does it make you feel closer to the biographer or does it bother you in some way? Does it give you a truer sense of history?

Reading with an Eye Toward Making Historical Thinking Visible for Students

Ever since Frank Smith first put forth the idea of "reading like a writer" (Smith, 1983), teachers and students have taken this idea to heart. This seemingly simple idea of finding all you need to know about writing in good literature has been the source of numerous minilessons, author studies, genre studies, and writing workshops. Katie Wood Ray's book *Wondrous Words* (1999) extends Smith's idea by providing a process for carefully examining literature, naming crafting techniques, and applying them as a writer.

This sensible idea of "reading like a writer" can be also applied to the study of biography. As we read, we can ask ourselves, What is the author doing that makes this such a good biography? Is the author telling us about using different sources of information, resolving conflicting accounts of events, and finding connections between past and present? What overall meaning is the author finding in this life story? What questions has the author raised that guided his or her research?

The examples of biographers' craft just discussed—Kathleen Krull's asking nosy questions, Russell Freedman's return to the same questions, Kathryn Lasky's asking lingering questions, and Diane Stanley's asking unanswerable questions—were discoveries I made while reading. The literature is full of these examples. But to find them, as we read biographies we need to pay attention to the opportunities they offer for discussing historical thinking. We need to ask, What information about historical thinking does this book have that I can share with my students? Out of this kind of reading will come discipline-specific questions like those raised in this book.

Why I Am Sold on a Questioning Approach to Biography

Once when I was teaching fifth grade I started the day by nonchalantly asking the class if they had any questions. Hands shot into the air. There was no input on my part, just a simple request for questions. I was startled by the results. Powerful questions were already present in my classroom.

I just hadn't realized it. And I hadn't realized how these questions could work for me and my students.

Through my experience with biography, I have learned about the importance of questions. A number of other educators have also stressed the importance of cultivating and using questions in the classroom. Stephanie Harvey in *Nonfiction Matters* (1998) suggests that we nurture students' compelling questions. Kathy Short, Jerome Harste, and Carolyn Burke in *Creating Classrooms for Authors and Inquirers* (1996) have explained that students need to have the time to find their own questions for inquiry to be meaningful. Isabel Beck, Margaret McKeown, Rebecca Hamilton, and Linda Kucan in *Questioning the Author* (1997) emphasize that through the use of open-ended questions—what they call queries or general probes—we "place the responsibility for thinking and building meaning on students" (p. 7), right where it belongs. I want to add my voice to theirs. But I also want to add that, at least in terms of history, we need to show students how to raise questions that are both compelling and discipline-specific. That is, we need questions that are not only interesting, but that promote historical thinking.

Questioning is essential to the teaching and learning of history. It's the antidote to history as archive, history as a one-way narrative, and history as "ironclad" in structure (Kincheloe, 2001, p. 592). Prompting students to ask *What if? What's the difference? What do I think?* and *What else?* when reading biography is a way to begin making history more of a process and less of an archive. Biography, with its compelling stories of individuals, is excellent material for questioning. Students can learn quite early that the essence of biography is "how one person sees and tries to understand another person's life and work" (Meltzer, 1985, p. 58). Other people might see that life and work quite differently. We have no reason to wait until students are in graduate school to learn this, since elementary school children grasp this idea with ease. In fact, they enjoy taking a questioning approach to biography.

Asking *What if? What's the difference? What do I think?* and *What else?* can lead to asking other questions like *Says who? So what? Why then? What caused . . . ? How is that event similar to . . . ?* and *How important is . . . ?* We can raise questions about historical context, perspective, cause and effect, and significance. Even more questions might follow. The essential point is that learning about biography, in the end, means learning to interrogate information. Do you have any questions?

REFERENCES

Atkins, J. (2002). "Did That Really Happen? Blurring the Boundary Between Fiction and Fact." *Book Links* 11: 30–31.

Bain, R. B. (2000). "Into the Breach: Using Research and Theory to Shape History Instruction." In P. N. Stearns, P. Seixas, and S. Wineburg (eds.), *Knowing, Teaching, and Learning History: National and International Perspectives* (331–52). New York: New York University Press.

Barton, K. (200l). "A Picture's Worth: Analyzing Historical Photographs in the Elementary School." *Social Education* 65: 278–83.

———. (1997). "'I just kinda know': Elementary Students' Ideas About Historical Evidence." *Theory and Research in Social Education* 25: 407–30.

Beck, I. L., M. G. McKeown, R. L. Hamilton, and L. Kucan. (1997). *Questioning the Author: An Approach for Enhancing Student Engagement with Text.* Newark, DE: International Reading Association.

Carvajal, D. (1998, February 24). "Now! Read the True (More or Less) Story!" *New York Times,* E1, E4.

Colman, P. (1999). "Nonfiction is Literature, Too." *The New Advocate* 12: 215–23.

Cowley, R. (ed.). (1999). *What If? The World's Foremost Military Historians Imagine What Might Have Been.* New York: Berkley/Penguin.

Crismore, A. (1984). "The Rhetoric of Textbooks: Metadiscourse." *Journal of Curriculum Studies* 16: 279–96.

Crismore, A., and W. J. Vande Kopple. (1988). "Readers' Learning from Prose: The Effects of Hedges." *Written Communication* 5: 184–202.

Cummins, J. (1998). "Storyographies: A New Genre?" *School Library Journal* 44: 42.

Curcio, F. R., M. Zarnowski, and S. Vigliarolo, S. (1995). "Mathematics and Poetry: Problem Solving in Context." *Teaching Children Mathematics* 1: 370–74.

Cushman, K. (2001). *Author Profile.* In S. Lehr (ed.), *Beauty, Brains, and Brawn: The Construction of Gender in Children's Literature* (99–103). Portsmouth, NH: Heinemann.

Davidson, J. W., and M. H. Lytle. (1992). *After the Fact: The Art of Historical Detection*. New York: McGraw-Hill.

Dooling, M. (2000). Artist's note. In J. C. Giblin, *The Amazing Life of Benjamin Franklin* (46). New York: Scholastic.

Dresang, E. T. (1999). *Radical Change: Books for Youth in a Digital Age.* New York: H. W. Wilson

Dresang, E. T., and K. McClelland. (1999). "Radical Change: Digital Age Literature and Learning." *Theory into Practice* 38: 160–67.

Edinger, M. (2000). *Seeking History; Teaching with Primary Sources in Grades 4–6.* Portsmouth, NH: Heinemann.

Ferguson, N. (ed.). (1997). *Virtual History: Alternatives and Counterfactuals.* New York: Basic Books.

Freedman, R. (2002). "A Conversation with Russell Freedman." In D. L. Darigan, M. O. Tunnell, and J. S. Jacobs (eds.), *Children's Literature: Engaging Teachers and Children in Good Books* (390). Upper Saddle River, NJ: Merrill.

———. (2000). "Bringing Them Back Alive: Writing History and Biography for Young Audiences." *Riverbank Review* 3: 19–22.

———. (1994). "Writing History and Biography for Young People." *School Library Journal* 40(3): 138–41.

Fritz, J. (2001). Nonfiction 1999. In M. Zarnowski, J. M. Jensen, and R. M. Kerper. (eds.), *The Best in Children's Nonfiction: Reading, Writing, and Teaching Orbis Pictus Award Books* (87–89). Urbana, IL: National Council of Teachers of English.

Grant, S. G. (2001). "It's Just the Facts, or Is It? Teachers' Practices and Students' Understandings of History." *Theory and Research in Social Education* 29: 65–108.

Harris, V. J., and S. J. McCarthey. (2002). "A Conversation with James Cross Giblin." *The New Advocate* 15: 175–82.

Harvey, S. (1998). *Nonfiction Matters: Reading, Writing, and Research in Grades 3–8.* York, ME: Stenhouse.

Holt, T. (1990). *Thinking Historically: Narrative, Imagination, and Understanding*. New York: College Entrance Examination Board.

Jensen, J. (2001). "The Quality of Prose in Orbis Pictus Award Books." In M. Zarnowski, R. M. Kerper, and J. M. Jensen (eds.), *The Best in Children's Nonfiction: Reading, Writing, and Teaching Orbis Pictus Award Books.* (3–12). Urbana, IL: National Council of Teachers of English.

Kerper, R. (In press). "Choosing Quality Nonfiction Literature: Examining Access Feathers and Visual Displays." In R. A. Bamford and J. V. Kristo (eds.), *Making Facts Come Alive: Choosing Quality Nonfiction Literature K–8.* (2nd ed.). Norwood, MA: Christopher-Gordon.

Kerper, R. M. (2000). "Excavating Voices, Illuminating History: A Conversation with Jim Murphy." *The New Advocate* 13: 117–27.

Kincheloe, J. L. (2001). *Getting Beyond the Facts: Teaching Social Studies/ Social Sciences in the Twenty-First Century.* New York: Peter Lang.

Krull, K. (1999). "Writing Biographies for Inquiring Minds." *Book Links* 8: 21–23.

Levstik, L. S., and D. B. Smith. (1996). "I've Never Done This Before: Building a Community of Historical Inquiry in a Third-Grade Classroom." In J. Brophy (ed.), *Advances in Research on Teaching: Vol. 6. Teaching and Learning History* (85–114). Greenwich, CT: JAI Press.

Lindquist, T. (1997). *Ways That Work: Putting Social Studies Standards into Practice*. Portsmouth, NH: Heinemann.

MacLeod, A. S. (1998). "Writing Backward: Modern Models in Historical Fiction." *The Horn Book* 74: 26–33.

Marcus, L. S. (2000). *Author Talk*. New York: Simon & Schuster.

Meltzer, M. (1989). "The Designing Narrator." In C. F. Otten and G. D. Schmidt (eds.), *The Voice of the Narrator in Children's Literature* (333–36). Westport, CT: Greenwood.

Moline, S. (1995). *I See What You Mean: Children at Work with Visual Information*. York, ME: Stenhouse.

Ott, B. (2002). "Spotlight on Biography." *Booklist* 98: 1281.

Overbye, D. (2002). "In the Beginning . . . and the Middle, and the End: New Data in Hand, Cosmologists Form a Grand Theory of the Universe." *New York Times* (23 July) F1, F6–7.

Parker, W. C. (2001). *Social Studies in Elementary Education* (11th ed.). Upper Saddle River, NJ: Merrill/Prentice Hall.

Paxton, R. J. (1999). "A Deafening Silence: History Textbooks and the Students Who Read Them." *Review of Educational Research* 69: 315–39.

———. (1997). "'Someone with Like a Life Wrote It': The Effects of a Visible Author on High School History Students." *Journal of Educational Psychology* 89: 235–50.

Percoco, J. A. (2001). *Divided We Stand: Teaching About Conflict in U.S. History*. Portsmouth, NH: Heinemann.

Perini, R. L. (2002). "The Pearl in the Shell: Author's Notes in Multicultural Children's Literature." *Reading Teacher* 55: 428–31.

Portalupi, J., and R. Fletcher. (2001). *Nonfiction Craft Lessons: Teaching Information Writing K–8*. Portland, ME: Stenhouse.

Rafael, T. (1986). "Teaching Question-Answer Relationships." *Reading Teacher* 39: 516–20.

Ray, K. W. (1999). *Wondrous Words: Writers and Writing in the Elementary Classroom*. Urbana, IL: National Council of Teachers of English.

Seidman, R. F. (2002). "Making Historical Connections." *School Library Journal* 48: 36–37.

Seixas, P. (2000). "Schweigen! Die Kinder! Or, Does Postmodern History Have a Place in Schools?" In P. N. Stearns, P. Seixas, and S. Wineburg (eds.), *Knowing, Teaching, and Learning History: National and International Perspectives* (19–37). New York: New York University Press.

Shemilt, D. (2000). "The Caliph's Coin: The Currency of Narrative Frameworks in History Teaching." In P. N. Stearns, P. Seixas, and S.

Wineburg (eds.), *Knowing, Teaching, and Learning History: National and International Perspectives* (83–101). New York: New York University Press.

Short, K. G., J. C. Harste, and C. Burke. (1996). *Creating Classrooms for Authors and Inquirers*. (2nd ed.). Portsmouth, NH: Heinemann.

Smith, F. (1983). "Reading Like a Writer." *Language Arts* 60: 558–67.

Stanley, D. (1988). "Picture Book History." *The New Advocate* 1: 209–20.

Tally, S. (2000). *Almost America: From the Colonists to Clinton: A "What If" History of the U.S.* New York: Quill/HarperCollins.

Trofanenko, B. (2002). "Images of History in Middle-Grade Social Studies Trade Books." *The New Advocate* 15: 129–32.

VanSledright, B. (2002). *In Search of America's Past: Learning to Read History in Elementary School.* New York: Teachers College Press.

VanSledright, B., and J. Brophy. (1992). "Storytelling, Imagination, and Fanciful Elaboration in Children's Historical Reconstructions." *American Educational Research Journal* 29: 837–59.

VanSledright, B., and C. Kelly. (1998). "Reading American History: The Influence of Multiple Sources on Six Fifth Graders." *Elementary School Journal* 98: 239–65.

Werner, W. (2000). "Reading Authorship into Texts." *Theory and Research in Social Education* 28: 193–213.

Welton, D. A. (2002). *Children and Their World: Strategies for Teaching Social Studies*. (7th ed.). Boston: Houghton Mifflin.

Wilson, S. L. (2001). *Coherence and Historical Understanding in Children's Biography and Historical Nonfiction Literature: A Content Analysis of Selected Orbis Pictus Books.* Unpublished doctoral dissertation. University of Maine, Orono.

Wineburg, S. (1999). "Historical Thinking and Other Unnatural Acts." *Phi Delta Kappan* 80: 488–99.

Wineck, H. (2001). "Yale and the Price of Slavery." *New York Times* (18 Aug.) A15.

Zarnowski, M. (In press). "It's More Than Dates and Places: How Nonfiction Contributes to Understanding Social Studies." In R. A. Bamford and J. V. Kristo (eds.), *Making Facts Come Alive: Choosing Quality Nonfiction Literature K–8* (2nd ed.). Norwood, MA: Christopher-Gordon.

———. (2001). "Intermingling Fact and Fiction." In M. Zarnowski, R. M. Kerper, and J. M. Jensen (eds.), *The Best in Children's Nonfiction: Reading, Writing, and Teaching Orbis Pictus Award Books* (13–21). Urbana, IL: National Council of Teachers of English.

———. (1997). "Interpreting Critical Issues: Comparing Past and Modern Plagues." *Social Studies and the Young Learner* 10: 10–13.

———. (1990). *Learning About Biographies: A Reading-and-Writing Approach for Children*. Urbana, IL: National Council of Teachers of English and the National Council for the Social Studies.

Children's Literature

Adler, D. (1990). *A Picture Book of Benjamin Franklin*. Illustrated by J. Wallner and A. Wallner. New York: Holiday House.

Aliki. (1999). *William Shakespeare & the Globe*. New York: HarperCollins.

Anderson, M. T. (2001). *Handel, Who Knew What He Liked*. Illustrated by K. Hawkes. Cambridge, MA: Candlewick.

Avi. (1990). *The True Confessions of Charlotte Doyle*. New York: Orchard.

Bisel, S. C. (1990). *The Secrets of Vesuvius: Exploring the Mysteries of an Ancient Buried City*. New York: Scholastic/Madison Press.

Blumberg, R. (1998). *What's the Deal? Jefferson, Napoleon, and the Louisiana Purchase*. Washington, DC: National Geographic Society.

Borden, L. (1999). *A. Lincoln and Me*. Illustrated by T. Lewin. New York: Scholastic.

Bridges, R. (1999). *Through My Eyes*. New York: Scholastic.

Corey, S. (2000). *You Forgot Your Skirt, Amelia Bloomer*. Illustrated by C. McLauren. New York: Scholastic.

Cox, C. (2001). *Houdini: Master of Illusion*. New York: Scholastic.

Christensen, B. (2001). *Woody Guthrie: Poet of the People*. New York: Knopf.

Fleischman, J. (2002). *Phineas Gage: A Gruesome but True Story About Brain Science*. Boston: Houghton.

Fradin, D. B. (1996). *"We Have Conquered Pain:" The Discovery of Anesthesia*. New York: McElderry/Simon & Schuster.

Fradin, D. B., and J. B. Fradin. (2000). *Ida B. Wells: Mother of the Civil Rights Movement*. New York: Clarion.

Freedman, R. (1999). *Babe Didrikson Zaharias: The Making of a Champion*. New York: Clarion.

———. (1987). *Lincoln: A Photobiography*. New York: Clarion.

———. (1961). *Teenagers Who Made History*. Illustrated by A. Shilstone. New York: Holiday House.

Fritz, J. (1976). *What's the Big Idea, Ben Franklin?* Illustrated by M. Tomes. New York: Coward, McCann & Geoghegan.

Fritz, J. (1969). *George Washington's Breakfast*. Illustrated by P. Galdone. New York: Putnam.

Giblin, J. C. (2000). *The Amazing Life of Benjamin Franklin*. Illustrated by M. Dooling. New York: Scholastic.

———. (1995). *When Plague Strikes: The Black Death, Smallpox, AIDS*. Illustrated by D. Frampton. New York: HarperCollins.

———. (1992). *George Washington: A Picture Book Biography*. Illustrated by M. Dooling. New York: Scholastic.

Gold, A. L. (2000). *A Special Fate: Chiune Sugihara: Hero of the Holocaust*. New York: Scholastic.

Handford, M. (1997). *Where's Waldo: The Wonder Book*. Cambridge, MA: Candlewick.

Harness, C. (2001). *Remember the Ladies: 100 Great American Women*. New York: HarperCollins.

———. (1998). *Ghosts of the White House*. New York: Simon & Schuster.

Holmes, T. (1998). *Fossil Feud: The Rivalry of the First American Dinosaur Hunters*. Parsippany, NJ: Messner.

Jaffe, S. H. (1996). *Who Were the Founding Fathers?: Two Hundred Years of Reinventing American History*. New York: Holt.

Josephson, J. P. (1997). *Mother Jones: Fierce Fighter for Workers' Rights*. Minneapolis, MN: Lerner.

Kostyal, K. M. (1999). *Trial by Ice: A Photobiography of Sir Ernest Shackleton*. Washington, DC: National Geographic Society.

Kraft, B. H. (1995). *Mother Jones: One Woman's Fight for Labor*. New York: Clarion.

Krull, K. (2000). *Lives of Extraordinary Women: Rulers, Rebels (and What the Neighbors Thought)*. Illustrated by K. Hewitt. San Diego: Harcourt.

———. (1998). *Lives of the Presidents: Fame, Shame (and What the Neighbors Thought)*. Illustrated by K. Hewitt. San Diego: Harcourt.

———. (1997). *Lives of the Athletes: Thrills, Spills (and What the Neighbors Thought)*. Illustrated by K. Hewitt. San Diego: Harcourt.

———. (1995). *Lives of the Artists: Masterpieces, Messes (and What the Neighbors Thought)*. Illustrated by K. Hewitt. San Diego: Harcourt.

———. (1994). *Lives of the Writers: Comedies, Tragedies (and What the Neighbors Thought)*. Illustrated by K. Hewitt. San Diego: Harcourt.

———. (1993). *Lives of the Musicians: Good Times, Bad Times (and What the Neighbors Thought)*. Illustrated by K. Hewitt. San Diego: Harcourt.

Lasky, K. (2000). *Vision of Beauty: The Story of Sarah Breedlove Walker*. Illustrated by N. Bennett. Cambridge, MA: Candlewick.

———. (1994). *The Librarian Who Measured the Earth*. Illustrated by K. Hawkes. Boston: Little, Brown.

MacLachlan, P. (1985). *Sarah, Plain and Tall*. New York: Harper & Row.

MacLeod, E. (1999). *Alexander Graham Bell: An Inventive Life*. Toronto: Kids Can.

Macy, S. (2001). *Bull's-Eye: A Photobiography of Annie Oakley*. Washington, DC: National Geographic Society.

Martin, J. B. (1998). *Snowflake Bentley*. Illustrated by M. Azarian. Boston: Houghton Mifflin.

Meltzer, M. (1998). *Ten Queens: Portraits of Women of Power*. Illustrated by B. Andersen. New York: Dutton.

———. (1985). *Dorothea Lange: Life Through the Camera*. Illustrated by D. Diamond. Photographs by D. Lange. New York: Viking Kestrel.

Mochizuki, K. (1997). *Passage to Freedom: The Sugihara Story*. Illustrated by D. Lee. New York: Lee & Low.

Murphy, J. (2000). *Pick & Shovel Poet: The Journeys of Pascal D'Angelo*. New York: Clarion.

———. (1995). *The Great Fire*. New York: Scholastic.
———. (1993). *Across America on an Emigrant Train*. New York: Clarion.
Myers, W. D. (2000). *Malcolm X: A Fire Burning Brightly*. Illustrated by L. Jenkins. New York: HarperCollins.
———. (1999). *At Her Majesty's Request: An African Princess in Victorian England*. New York: Scholastic.
Partridge, E. (2002). *This Land Was Made for You And Me: The Life and Songs of Woody Guthrie*. New York: Viking.
Pelta, K. (1991). *Discovering Christopher Columbus: How History Was Invented*. Minneapolis: Lerner.
Pinkney, A. D. (1998). *Duke Ellington: The Piano Prince and His Orchestra*. New York: Hyperion.
Rappaport, D. (2001). *Martin's Big Words: The Life of Dr. Martin Luther King, Jr.* Illustrated by B. Collier. New York: Hyperion.
Rockwell, A. (2000). *Only Passing Through: The Story of Sojourner Truth*. Illustrated by R. G. Christie. New York: Knopf.
Sís, P. (1996). *Starry Messenger: A Book Depicting the Life of a Famous Scientist, Mathematician, Astronomer, Philosopher, Physicist, Galileo Galilei*. New York: Farrar Straus Giroux.
Stanley, D. (1998). *Joan of Arc*. New York: William Morrow.
———. (1996). *Leonardo da Vinci*. New York: William Morrow.
———. (1986). *Peter the Great*. New York: William Morrow.
Stanley, D., and P. Vennema. (1994). *Cleopatra*. Illustrated by D. Stanley. New York: William Morrow.
———. (1992). *Bard of Avon: The Story of William Shakespeare*. Illustrated by D. Stanley. New York: William Morrow.
———. (1988). *Shaka: King of the Zulus*. Illustrated by D. Stanley. New York: William Morrow.
Stanley, J. (2000). *Hurry Freedom: African Americans in Gold Rush California*. New York: Crown.
Szabo, C. (1997). *Sky Pioneer: A Photobiography of Amelia Earhart*. Washington, DC: National Geographic Society.